I0490529

It Is I

DALE MIKELS

authorHOUSE®

AuthorHouse™
1663 Liberty Drive
Bloomington, IN 47403
www.authorhouse.com
Phone: 833-262-8899

Published by AuthorHouse 11/04/2020

ISBN: 978-1-6655-0639-7 (sc)
ISBN: 978-1-6655-0638-0 (e)

Library of Congress Control Number: 2020921679

Print information available on the last page.

It is I That I see
In the Mind of mE
It iS I thAt is writTen
For the Truth to unfOld
Forsaken IN spirIt
BelliGerent iN mInd
It is I That I see

Autumn 1978

CHAPTER ONE

It Is I...

It began as a joke, this extra end of ours but, never being much of a savant for languages, as far as the composition of sentences is concerned, I wouldn't be able to tell you which, in my opening dialogue, is the predicate of the purpose for this writing. The subject, itself, is a joke. The adjective will be any descriptive nomenclature my cursor can conjure. Personally, the word splat! comes to mind, for actionary scripture, but that may be my glass half-full mentality speaking it's mind, too. I can tell you all designations are germaine but, as individuals, none fully describe life's situation, as we know it.

Seventyfour years ago, a small gathering took place after a prom, in Hivicksburg, South Afrika. There were many celebrations taking place in the region during that same week but, it wasn't a difficult search to locate, isolate, and then terminate the two young men who, because of their antics, started the (yes, extra) end we are experiencing. Taking a breath is standard practice before diving into the abyss, so

Give me a second

And, the discovery of an open door in a chromosome, gave the sciences new theories to confirm; the one of interest being, the Catorstrum theorem. It being associated with genetic tracing but, it also innocently suggested the possibility of coding and upgrading strings of DNA, all by remote access, which could benefit man's intellectual and physical progression throughout the universe. The basic understanding was that we could alter our sequence, en route, making deep space exploration, and our survivability of it, a more probable adventure. That's how it was sold to the public, anyways. With a billion dollar marketing firm painting the picture, we agreed, again, with the premise of the research being 'harmless', to us. We failed to not mention any side effects, leaking everywhere, the voluntarily influenced had experienced, while being experimented upon, again, with our blessing

Notice the similarities of the X words

They are vewy similar
Yet different

Our experiences are fresh and exciting, and, sometimes, make us what we are but, if our experiments are successful; you liked it; you've expanded a border with the experience. If it will be your last breath before you will ever place that vileness anywhere near a great idea, and allow the memories to slowly dissolve into what would be a great idea

Free your mind

The same genius had sold the far gone electorate on the safety of the Padrick Electron Accelerator humanity was given years before; which never have created black holes large enough to be of any concern but, when opposing ions are sent on an apparent collision course with destiny, in machines that are, by testimony, anciently state-of-the-art and ill-maintained: and yes, I said, again; there is always the slightest opportunity for a disaster to unfurl.

The first 'exercise', at the 'plant', did 'nothing' but grant the science world 'a spectacular show' but, not wanting to miss an ounce of time and, them not getting the results they prewanted, their second attempt gave everyone a good show, and was registered as 'ab', sending a blooming mushroom twenty miles at its apex, and, 'allegedly' unleashing the largest thunderstorm storm ever seen on our surface. Bertha, she's called, now circles the earth every forty-three to forty-four days, depending on her rooster tail, and is only a concern, to date, if you choose to live halfway around the world.

The clean-up afterwards, of what was reportedly not another attempt to gain the wisdom of our father's father father,

'It lives!' He screamed, laughing madly.

During what was building upstairs; she wasn't full strength, yet, but, when she was receiving her wings and was beginning to be gone; she was then added to the back-burner list, becoming a moot point, after crews' began disappearing on site. Six crews, consisting of fifty apiece, that being in two sets; one, a supplemental reinforcement; and the search crews of thrice the number made a couple best-sellers, a while back. They All Went Away.

No one was left, however, to be witness to anything, with exception of the last volunteer search battalion sent in to recon the original blast zone. They reported and evidenced the zone's condition, as did their comrades earlier in the month, who also gave the all-clear from within the rubble. The addendum log, submitted by the second recon team, had the entry of what was described as '…items considered to be foreign to the human body, i.e., clothing, jewelry, dental work, tattoos, toupees, etc'. A friend of mine joked, adding 'brain' to the list, when he gave the Chamber a synopsis of the historical story. I bought Max a couple drinks because of the first time he gave me the **going back to the** party **in three two**

I'm a squirt
Not a big Squirt
Just a Squirt
One of the last
Remaining Squirt's there is
Our pool ran dry
With the feuds
And all
The feuds was about the Squirts'
And the Rubbishes'
Meandering careers
As bodyguards to the stars
To where the Squirt's didn't want
to sit Amongst the Rubbish
And the Rubbish's felt the Squirts
Were blowing
The whole affair out of proportion
(**STREAKY CLAT**ter noise plays)
(**A GENTLE WO**mans voice plays)

This has been a test
Of the emergency actuary
Program
If you haven't lived yet

It had lasted for hours, as the young and freshly educated over-indulged in spirits, making several, as you might guess, bolder than when the festivities first began. The celebratory atmosphere eventually brought an overly-intoxicated innocent, hereafter, known as, Mr. Yeller Godiva, into two mens 'let's tie him to a mule and send it out' comedic endeavor, and, into what is now understood as, a pulse of the zone. It, the Zone, is another migraine of the aforementioned big bang catastrophe, and has been described as a 'collateral effect', also, of the initial collider explosion. Instead of moving away and building, the Zone was born and bred at ground zero.

The Zone, unlike Bertha, with her mass and her unwavering line of travel; an equatorial, energy building paradise; is an invisible entity, still, whom, forgive the life-giving pronoun, is mobile and shifts from one location to another, and remaining in unpopulated areas for the same amount of time it takes big B to revolve our circumference. Whatever it is, it has monitoring skills, made apparent by its freely crossing into the south, without fear of friends, while other vessels within range will be the victims of flybys on land, with twice the approach speed at sea. We've almost got the best of it, if you call almost the best ya' got.

Several researchers, without voluntary guard, had attempted up close and personal studies of the unusual phenomena; performing the usual specimen sampling, if any have been been taken; size estimations, energy exchanges, and et cetera; but, after the first guinea pig disappeared, leaving behind holstered equipment, too, with hollowed-out clothing attached; all seen and reported by the second squeaker who was ordered in to accomplish the original task, before her vanishing confirmed that any remaining evaluations should be taken by a satellite, far, far away.

A thinner Godiva had returned hours after his departure, with the mule's empty bridle in his hands, and expressing gratitude for the delicacy; his translation. The foreign language the virgin had begun to speak was automatic knowledge gained by all within earshot; and one foreign, eventually, to everyone who knew anything about the ancient tongues; and/or, the blue-eyed and yellowish shimmering birthday suit, uh, young Yeller served us, are three answers' we seek.

Godiva eventually responded to fan mail shortly after its arrival, and with making additional deposits at the 'light company', or, he, himershe had a good thought and was merely locating desired genetic codes; for what purpose, no one knows.

The live broadcast, across USB airwaves, was made with no assistance needed, thank you, and became the fatal blow for the original duo of pranksters, coming as an electrostatic adjustment and furnished by the Genetic Alignment Program; GAP for short. It was exposed as a behind-the-scenes research investment, and a popularly funded monogram for our leaders. Once nucleic acid databases were uploaded to a centralized location, GAP HQ; because of an undying thirst to know our own heritage, databases thrive, in abundance, and, with their functionality sequences upgraded, making them transmission compatible, we became dots on a map. If you are a dot, that is. You, at night, with shadows vast, are a barely noticeable lighter shade of grey bleeping off in the flicker of a Neosun sunset.

"The universal broadcast became a pandemic and released through the metaphysical and upon those who had been touched..."

As Max continued reciting the story, my thoughts hemorrhaged, remembering both, my first attempts of trying to make it through that sentence, and calculating superluminal formulas *don't say a word but i rented out the ciphering for the book Max is reading* is an incredible task, involving loads of research. *Plus, oh, sorry*

Plus
It gave me a headache

With my friend entertaining the rubble of the Chamber, by reciting the rubble of my first published chronicles, which featured what man has swept away; my first real realization, with the toll the three unexplainable disasters have taken, equalling a third of the populous but, it became a better conversation piece when it morphed into being a challenge to the GAP alignment, to decode the code that created the flesh-eating, and dropless, blob.

The 'Touch' has never been eradicated, thanks to the Alliance, GAP, because it would create a discussion of legalities, for possessing it, or, to isolate the open door, which creates catastrophes, and to be able to put a rise in the recoding of us

237378

Once the 'remotely controlled' idea came, by sheer genius, and then perfected; two movers~and~shakers got together to make a cheaper, more generic version of the remotely controlled access unit. At cut-rate prices, it came without Big G's bells and whistles, but law abiding citizens were the smart ones, they stood still; knowing, while the others flinch

> *You kids gotta go*
> *To Grandma for treats*
> *We other's count*

After several years, a decision was made to cancel Godiva's, 'Neon R It', lifetime subscription. The Politios hoped this would solve the problem but, after all avenues of annihilation were exhausted; including an attack of the successful GAP program, which only caused the death of twelve scientists; the powers' circled their wagons, again, and declared the project a *long-term investment strategy.*

The Zone retaliated with multiple eruptions, some stretching for miles, at times, from it's outer rim. These protrusions caused the death rate to skyrocket, with the reciprocal occurring in the value of used clothing apparel.

This newest form of yellow fever has now lasted over seventy years, is untraceable, impossible to isolate or penetrate, they found, and it isn't an air-bourne pathogen, doubland, never has it's namesakes hue, until it comes into contact with the human condition. Including a reddish ring around the collar, that no cleanser can repair, which is how one knows when you've been had. By the time you make a list of all that, it's too late. It's known, in the media, as the faceless hangman.

As I sauntered over to the postal receptacle; yes, they're still here, I'd be too, if my family purchased three million dollar homes; I spotted another Politio adverb hanging loosely by a thread, as far as my eyes could see. Pulling it, as if their disease will touch me, their letters began to appear:

~Thank you for survivability! I'd appreciate your support in Neyvember!~ The Party's encouragement pushed the last button. It was time.

Droplets of water, being born one second and smashing against my storm shield the next, pleaded for some semblance to an existence within my broken world. Their amphibious appendages, in fascinating arrays, spread outwardly, in attempts to cling to any morsel of hope protruding from their smoothed landing surface. A solitary dribble, tiny as a newborn, rebelled against the status quo and scampered frantically upwards. It's arm arced forward, as double-bladed cleaners flawlessly pilfered away it's aspirations. I watched as the spirited one was swept off the edge, to rejoin it's comrades in their rebirth. A small aquatic mitten, with what amazingly looked like a hook attached, waved it's farewells.

I mimicked a shrug and waved back, before realizing it was a piece of water and I had given it what it wanted most of all.

Reality, my favorite of the three *check!* cleansed my dramatics by offering into view, and through precipitative turmoil, my most favored residential ecstasy. It's one of a few hospitable environments still struggling to maintain an air of functionality, and sits a couple plots down from the brick and mortar harbouring Max's Art & Amusement, my second choice as a final resting place. My mahal looked to have taken more of a beating from the recently passed storm; a ruptured blade is revolving, making itself nauseous.

Turbulence, in repetitive and frustrated bursts, made it's attempts at shattering the passenger side windows, while streaking streams of accumulated moisture horizontal, marring any clear view of my dream. It floats quietly past as; much to the shagrin *now* of oncoming traffic; my world contorts, transforming a wishful soul into a perfectly contoured grandfather rocker, who is brilliantly and majestically gift wrapped by an encircling veranda, with whitened aerators patiently circulating a soft, tantalizing breeze of quiet. Their peaceful zephyr doubly giving life to the surrounding blades of gently waving green, cascading to the horizons.

My homestead production, designed with a

combination of aboriginal Victorian schematics and Chelation chemology, grappled with its own survival. It's once elegant facade, racked again and again by an insistent foe, crumbles to pieces and returns itself to the dust from which it rose.

Attention alerts from my crew abruptly locked my vision onto the rearview, double checking what may have crept into the view of my lack of interest. It was clear, except for the dampened kamikaze's, who were countable only a few clicks earlier. With great delight, they sparkled in the moonlight, as their increase and strength became more evident, proven by the inundation of every porous condition in their path.

Pretend you're a bug going ten rounds in the battle of life. For them, during times like this, it serves them good purpose for there to be a few leaves remaining in the area to ward off the storm's persistence. Billions of years of natural living evolve the insect into a super species, conditioned to withstand both hell and high water but, we all could use a little help, from time to time. But, who stood in line the day the lottery went out, to pick who has to put up with us.

Take crocodilians, for instance, and put them in a cockroaches body, oh my. It is what the leaders want; but, a cockroach doesn't want to be their buddy, or yours, whether they be toothed, or not. Take the Ping

Pong Tree Sponge, it replanted itself atop our largest mountain range, to do what? Or, accomplish what? Even at eighty leagues down, And, who got the raw end of the deal on that one?

Now, switch the organisms, and play rocket-man with my little friend, or, take a selfie in the abyss but, it might be too cool to say, I have spicules!

The shower, come flood, was a spectacular sight. I wondered, outside of the surface climber, if the moistened molecules ever knew of their purpose; being born of the masses and ending an existence in a joint and singular attempt to give life elsewhere. I also wondered, 'Who loves ya, baby?', whether there was a pecking order to their madness as Mr. Telly Savalas, dreamlike in his quality, crooned encouraging sonnets to the voluntarily submitted liquids pooling beneath his digitally generated likeness. In the background, pressure-driven hatches silently and with rapture, slid open and closed, separating each bead from it's siblings, releasing all in timed rhythm to a gravitationally generated pulse, drawing them downward and into terminal velocity, just before impact; a carte du jour feast. My attention turned back to the task at hand; arriving my debilitation safely to its destination.

I felt better about life, if only slightly.

Amen, to the Upside-down Pale-faces, who chose

not to degrade their system, by replacing it's mascot, and naming themselves, the Team, instead.

eventually end up being absurd. If you don't believe that to be true, you, like I, should have thought of Timothy Dilons classic lyric

> *If an asshole has an opinion*
> *Does it need to make a sound*

A doubletake is a natural reaction from a guy who blinks but, instead of learning from our past, we tear down our lessons to it, and because of it, you rip it from my history book; a book which is made to be heard, and, we thought, understood? What's next

> *I'd like to know*
> *What*
> *My offspring is learning*

Where'd you hear that!?

We all have a history to point with, and people don't want to follow a god who gives free will, but they want to take mine away. Now, when we're strolling by an open space of air, and, somewhere in your parenting genes; maybe yesterday you heard a story about a life, about that horse's life, as the figure's were passed; you, maybe on a wishful stroll one day. And, sometimes a prodigy, being just high enough to reach the hoof of the next question, will have to develop their talent elsewhere, or, go ride one, before their time on earth is done. It's better to never take anything for granted, and it's never a bad thing to learn everything, while we can. So, why are you feeling yourself not a parent? Our character develops the next nation, the next life we will live or through, as it has from the beginning

An old friend would say
We are the village
I don't know what the festivities
Were back in the day
Dave
*(**NOISE OV**er crowd)*
But
Rumor has it
Word of mouth got involved
And the whole place went nuts

The only way to learn about anything, is to hear about it? We all know how good word of mouth is, and I pray, that, if that is the way we will hire our next party member, I pray I'm long gone before that squad takes the field. And, I'd be up to an idea of term limits; where three terms are served and three rewarding terms are paid for, and, their gold watch is the pension we are paid for the same job well done

Sure
I'll mail in that ballot

Who'd be behind that .. nauseous feeling when you've known of the train wreck, felt it from a distance, with multitudes never seeing its obvious translucence

Team
Mascot
Retired
Hall of Fame
For his life's battles
Trying to live on his land
And creating stuffs
To not have ufs

We are still encroaching on others, like we are accused of, taking what we want, designating, as we do; demanding change everywhere possible.

Why do we want everyone else to be like we are? When what we are, is being overtaken by anything with a plan, whether they're homegrown, or not. Their battle plan, clear by observation of the stars, for power is being unveiled right under our nose

The Squirt's and the Rush's
Come to mind

So, why would anyone want us to be a free and profitable land, ruled by the foreseers of the past, who wanted us a better life but, one slip, in human greed, from one, became an epidemic.

We know who the one was, and have allowed her to pass, by natural causes; peacefully, in her sleep. Instead of allowing GAP to be involved, which led me to believe that maybe our curse is tied to one, and we are to breed out the faithful, until we are left to the means of ourselves.

We will survive until whatever it's going to be takes us away, or out. As a human condition, survivability is a key instinct, and many have sustained themselves because of it.

Many have taught themselves out of believing in what I know. And, that is, He rose. It's what I put my faith in, and, understand the difference in having faith He rose, and knowing He did.

Commander Perry; who became our beloved second in line to marital aids, after a wedding to an already sitting Madame President; the leader the sobor of a different sort decided we should have.

She was gracious enough to wait for her *Honeymoon Of A Lifetime;* to be paid for by coffers, purchased by those of faceless descent; and forget the commander's insignia. Junior; see, even that gets a Big Letter; wears the brandishingly gooch *it's missing something* on every item of clothing anyone named Jangles would be proud to wear.

Just because he was an idiot before his nuptials; not nupchuals, as has been bred in me but, before the wedding

Me
What do I think
I think he's an embarrassment
Bringing Reality TV
And that do
To the Washed House

What has the 'Madame' been up to, prior to election

Can't say as I know
Youngun

Me and the Missus moved away from these parts, long a go. I can tell you what I heard

Iffin' thata be sumthin
Thata grab ya goozle

If we are labouring in our sweat, without adequate supplies; enough to not start eating Uncle Jake's cooking; we will never survive this, in an upright state, with us reaching the end of an end, at each end

Iffin it be crumbs you want
Crumbs ye get

Maybe catching a crumb or two on our way down might be ranked high on our list of options but, our fortitude is amazing, with our appetite for children, spitting and throwing understated expletives, all before an audience, which is what occurred during Madame Barbie's thrust for the reigns of puppet power

UNITE

The sixty-eight paralleled into a residual slot at that side of the broken roadway, which had been deteriorated by repetitive storm damage but, mainly, because of a lack of enthusiasm from the dedicated few road builders who remained in the area

UNITED

Or.

It became apparent that the article was not what was being looked for, Scavenger ran away as fast as she approached

So
In her rounds
She might run up on ya
When she runs
Watch

Her auburn hair sweeps to her sides *into particles of matter pulsing in rhythmic tunes* and swaying through her length, in slow motion, just like in the movies and pet food advertisements. Her laugh's as fun *as your mother-in-laws* to be around *as a grapefruit on a sunny day* as a gulf breeze on a chilly morning. That is, when your flesh doesn't boil on contact, which really is a contradictory comparison

HOT
COLD
RIMSHOT

She's a good one.

She was the kind of dog that is smarter than me, better looking than me, eats more than me, and sleeps more than me, which is possibly the best part about her. My friend likes her space, too, and, good thing for me, she's a tea-toteler.

Wishing to have her back doesn't change the simplest of realities, and as I progress through the years, I find it more difficult to say farewell to old friends, who both, at the time, know it is the last time. There's only one instance, where the word was never said

But
Ain't no reason
To go d'ere

Unfortunately, Cage, my pet name for her, saw me at my worst of times. She never paid for it, but you could tell. The darkness had taken something from her, but maybe it added noise sensitivity, too, which made her an excellent house grumble. She was always beside me, or not very far away, and, always, after sleeping, she'd come through, checking to see if we were all breathing. It's those times that I'll remember about her, when she proved she was better at this life-thing than me.

If my project had taken me to depths unknown, or to more fundamental actions, like, rubbing a chin, biting a pencil, resting my finger on my lips, ripping six inches of flesh away to reveal

I AM NOT A MACHINE
SEE

Or.

A holographic webbing, erected between batter

and pithcher, as unionized protection for the batter. It's proportions are calculated by a lifetime of at-bats by the guest player, and appears *sometimes as a fish* locked into position, with passage allowed through only one side. It's presence is disguised, plateside, with a see through keying effect, but with pornographic movies *pay attention* moundside.

When the thing goes haywire, on UTV; turning backwards, blinking, someone hacking it, *Your Mother Crazy*, or if it is functioning at all; one might think a perfected point might be gained before installation, but time is money, and

Have I got a
Great idea for you

The first time a one eighty took place, the batter was called out; for intruding with inanimate objects; which caused a scandal, which caused a rules change, which did nothing for the down and out batter. Who, by trajectory, again calculated by the forensic guys, would have won the game with the three ribi blast.

Thanks to GAP legislation, which led to the overtake of all laboratories, forensic medicine has changed through the years, causing every graduate to redial their talents. And, wasting the passion was not an option for several scientific types, who were famously appearing on postal service bulletins universally, when a short term genetic cure had been developed.

They adapted, those who already had training and abilities elsewhere, and became inventive in honest life, making survivability a top priority.

Being inventive, in very many ways and places, is not, and will not be the downfall of us. It might show our character, or, sometimes following what seemed to be important *only moments ago*

Finally
We come to our senses

Or.

It took The Yackie to open the door, and Sun to open the mind, to prove we are not who we are telling each other we are. And many for years have stated, proven by fact, the same truth we've mocked, and hung from a tree. When we knew.

Fear is a strong, bolstering emoticon, used to spread gossip, to instill alarm in those wanting to buy their own tickets, because *something needs to be done.*

Living off the land, never knowing if it will offer nourishment, but grateful for a nearby stream, will change a person into one or the other. It's up to them as to which passion will control their life

Mine
You know
Every move you make
Rollercoasta'
Of love
Rainy day on Munday

I am not aware of any diseases by contact, or god curses, that have been sparked, because of interracial breeding but, some have rumored, it was us who created the famous epidemics of our past; we, disturbing the species of the deep.

Which doesn't explain

Why were spots
Around the globe
Bombed

Looking on the map for impact zones is the easiest observational, ever.

If hadaled sea creatures, unknown to us, have tapped into their underwater guests; seismic sensors, communications webs, etc.; they know everything we know, and, how would we know of their technology? We don't even know if they exist.

GAP produced another observational of interest, it contained charted locations of our sequential beginnings, and, proved a second splurge of creation located within the Realms, where we are told we are from

We are one
Race

Not a group of separate races trying to kill the other because of a belief, or loathing the other because of an itch we can't quite scratch, or gluttony; binging on one another and having an appetite for it

Hmmm

And, if a man is true to his spiritual guidance, and follows a written word, he will fall, and lead more with IT. Having had literary greats among us, and every one striking me in my *wow* zones, but not one would I trust completely, with their direction for my life.

Do I need you to get where I'm going

Well no
But
You don't have to splash
Street muck on me
When you pass by

Because we are the same, we fight for ways to be different, and nothing will make us different. What makes us the same, above all, is what makes us liable for the care of one another, and, we're not adding to your grief, by adding one more thing to your day. If someone truly needs help, you'll know. You won't avoid the issue, and say

Why
I believe
Luvy
That that person
Might be of assistance
You'll do
What you can

Or.

The bright, multicolored lights of downtown, now seen above my ten and two positioning, were soundless in their presentation. My state of forward motion squeaked to a halt, as the steadily broken glint, catapulted off a gorged and saturated surface, sent me away. The euphoria created, even now, and magnified by traveling composites, was also a tremendous side attraction to the vestibule that leans on my little hill; which leans. If it were one and not both doing the leaning, I'd pick a card from the deck, and run for the door; I don't have enough to cover the tab

Maybe that's me

However, the jubilation and peace of an aura doesn't work as well in cold weather, doubland, flashing lights, as a couple strands do, take me back to a past best forgotten. So, if you might happen to be passing by a shivering old man, at night, shielding his molecular portals from the mind-controlling thumping noises, he's just trying to get to door number two.

I reached for the ignition and counter turned *check!* until *check one two!* the engine's subtle drone, not quite a chug, came to a breathing halt. Before retrieving the key, which would signal my internal to begin it's exit-the-car routine, instead, I listened to the rampaging troops hammering their objections against my roof, because of the placement of my auto vehicle. They do speak, the drops, as various, now erect animals do but, with a language unresolved, and one can only assume the present heart-to-heart.

My intellect squealed, as it began reading the last known posted note, 'Go with the mutton chops'; but, the intellect is under review, and, under parameter's and safe-guard's data upgrades, leaving a strain on it, I now plead, causing it to whimper, most grotesquely; it not believing it would be his duty to not throw out the trash, as a normally functioning unit might. It would attempt to do the trash taking out kinda dance but, intelligence didn't have the legs to stand in line until he got a pair of his own *So you can*

Win
1000000000 dollars

Now, forgetting an object's location *You two stop it* means it's lost, yes? Until it's found, of course *sorry boss.*

If never found, it's category is forever lost. It is mine, but, it's possession has changed geographic locations

Simple

If, at some point, the memory recalls the item's location, or, we just happen to come across it, or, I dropped it, or et freaking cetera

Now
Re-read that
With more drama this time
A Shitner impersonation
Would be cool
For fellow trek-a-moniacs
And find the comma I just placed
While practicing

It's always a joyus, roasting a prodigal one, kind of celebration, as the mind ages, quicker in some, sorry. It loses items on an uninterrupted basis but, the search for what is known lost, that intuition, is made even more difficult, when my possession of a piece of it is unknown to me to begin with

> *There were*
> *Undetected derailments*
> *With the sismo trains*

About the same time as the derailments, with my involvement being minimal, and with the rebellion, from the last time I interfered with interest

> *Got a memo I found*
> *Amongst a stash of mail parked*
> *just behind my eyes*
> *You know where they hit cha'*
> *Square*

It had something to do with track crossings, so, I just assumed someone else would do the painting; as I started work on a project that would identify whatever was going to paint my(?) crosswalk

> *Why is there a*
> *Big S painted on that one*

How many people does it take to create a need for a crosswalk *and* memorizing anything above a consonant, under my presently normal physiological conditions, is flipping on the side of fantastical feats **has moved to**

It's new night
And new time

Barring any cranial refurbishments and upgrades, observational failures can be eliminated if incoming data were correctly transcoded

Vital subject
Break
Transmittal code
(**SNAP**rebuttalTwo)
Phantom
Charles Xavier
Uranus
Pudgy
(#!?$+|° plays)

Which would alert Operator #Δ64 to catalog areas, where there are ongoing schematic upgrades, transposed under orbonic lighting

(**HEAVY BRE**athing plays)

They are to put together a survivability approximation, in case, but, I dare anyone to walk into that cubicle, it is spotless, but, who knows what's supposed to go where.

Take for instance, the high resonance evacuator, taking up space in my θ quadrant, didn't have a cute curly Q, yesterday. I'm not sure if I should take that as the Q replacing the /- on the previous upgrade, or is it the Q, reappearing, after it was replaced by the /-? The /-? is smiling at you, from someone you may know.

Portals are where vacations are made for the mind and it's individual departments, at their leisure, to enjoy the good life, if only for a few days. In case informational processes became needed and extras, in the good ole days crew masters would preload pods and store information on-site, as backup, before they spun off the dock.

Presently, the crews are having to recharge enough to alert itself to unhook, first, to be able to recharge. Though, having never been witness, if any are needed before compartments are completely rested, the crews will demand additional addictions, because it's just not right.

The undivulged locations of the said-to-be paradises are elsewhere in the galaxy, making their ascertainment accessible only to those with proper documentation, which must be dated prior to Buell's Day

> *I'm missing a stripe*
> *And*
> *Not allowed visitation rights*
> *So*

While we others walk down the halls of liberty, banging the gong of salutation, sorry; while we others hobble down the halls of liberty, uh, while we others trudge forth to a fate already decided; Ole Mr. Yeller is galavanting, in all his splendor, around the universe. Well, around us, maybe.

It's terrible and baffling to me, by what must be a territorial conflict. One sense is falling well short of expected goals, and obviously not gonna make the cut, while other 'under-achieving' obstacles rebel against a tyrannical methodology elected through attrition. Thus, having to adapt tried-and-true actions to compensate for reactions caused by a lack of uniformity, somewhere in the cosmos, and life goes from makin' it to *what am I doing exactly* in a millisecond. Age sometimes causes one to have too much to think about, which should justifiably be one single thought, or action, at any given moment; not the potential, or actual, train wreck foreseen with a solitary idea's Illumination

Thank you
The defense rests

With the cocoon's grace slowly leaking away and bringing us back to a dying age, we wait for an 'all systems go' signal from the chief mechanics, who will either allow the body to fluidly pass motion, or, because of some vindictive ulterior motive, an abundance of weighted material is distributed to random parts of the body

Where there are
Not supposed to be
Any vacancies
Causing a list in the already
Navigationally challenged

So, with the Major Advocate General's cross-training policy in hand, and backing me, I took the argument, for better dispensation procedures, upstairs. I had time to feel the temperature of the office doorknob before being turned around and ordered back to my post

Ok
You tell the mechanics
They are now engineers
RADoFonics is live
And stfu

Said it nicely
Congratulations Engies
We have a major recharting action
Needed from the engineering crew
Who will be manning station
ΩB Six
That's the overlook with all the
Spidder webs
Lookin like maps
Shaleetle
He or She will
Be responsible for
the Planning and the Development
Of conceptual maptifications
Presented
Upon these screens
In both
*Ex-pi-**eli**-n-ocious*
You're welcome
And Cartiagraphicus Cinema
Once properly trained
In about six seconds
At these essential procedures
They can just look down
And follow the lines
Like the others do

Servos were ladened with energy, and lubrication, weighing what felt like tons, was plopped onto and into skeletal junctions most in need, which was downplaying the process, all sections needed crooning. Mental alerts were sent to components deepest within our audience ***checkcheck*** asking of them ***systems three one and two*** fifteen percent more ***are in deactivation stage alpha*** attention than normally applied to ***audiokinetic slew rate adjusted to level pulse six*** this portion of the drive but, because of the present weather conditions, and, lately ***RADoFonicS will be live in three two one roll tape***

> (**A POPU**lar nite show topic plays)
> (**A GENTLE WO**man's voice plays)
> ***Automated shutdown sequence***
> ***initiated***
> (**GENER**ators begin shutting down)
> *Have we got clearance to use that*
> (**AN UNIN**telligible voice speaks)
> *I don't care what year it is*
> *Pick another one*

The inner tomb feels a chill, because of the present weather conditions, and lately ***RADoFonicS will be live in three two one roll tape***

(**A POPU**lar nite show topic plays)
(**A GENTLE WO**man's voice plays)
***Automated shutdown sequence
Initiated***
(**GENER**ators begin shutting down)
(+#¶¶¶¶¶¶¶¶¶¶+)
What do you Mean it's STuck
(**AN UNINTELLIGIBLE** voice speaks)

I visualized every digit of every geal-ending name, within every finger that thought better of themselves, and decided not to show up for the snails race, today.

As the key was withdrawn, and while the left quadrant stretched those geals, to their last ledge, filling, and feeling, the gaps of ones less interested, my memory wanders **RADoFonicS is live in**

Tonight on
Casper Goes To Col-
That's all you had
-lege
With raspberry pie
(**+&$#!!+**)
(**AN EXHALA**tion of breath plays)
(**+&$#!!+**)

A while back, this same scenario had led to a humongous debate amongst my upstairs peers. I was demoted because of it, a stripe less person, and have yet to regain the lost respect you should be caught up by now

(**WHIRR**ing engine noise plays)
Have you occupied the sanitary
extraction center yet?
(**&#!/%**)
I'm sorry
(××)
Of coursth I appealda, awgwuing
Lady
And gentleman
The tempting of fate
By only the fingertips
As we do
On a number of occasions
And us
Compensating for a crew
Who have grown tired
Long before I
Makes us grip objects
In a tighter fashion
Than was previously sufficient

Hence
Making my poor
Dismal agony worse
An Agony
Made worse again
By an internal reactionary system
Maintained
I am proud to say
At its highest possible levels

And, because of the uninstallable, and highly blockadedable, but highly obtainable 'holy crap' mode, when it initiates it's reactions to innocent actions, when nothing goes as planned

($&#√)
And
Lady and Gentleman
Far be it from me
To set forth in this argument
That
It is not
In the delegation's bylaws
That
I am to lose a stripe
Over this nature of infraction

And, *yes*! I know whining hour does not begin for another sixtyfour tip twelve nanoseconds.

It has always been entertaining having the only free, 'made in gold', backstage pass to the theater that is mine, isn't it? I lost the vote, as you recall, and another stripe, due to my *at-ti-tude*, the buggers. I don't know how much my loss came to, there is no corresponding or translatable counting system to speak of, because *they don't do numbers up there,* and

I do not want to know

As my head cleared it's thoughts, and my roof, the exit sequence was thankfully initiated without much over-thinking. It did become clearer that even more troops had been properly motivated for this, 'Blast The Old Guy' mission of theirs. My shoulders and head, only just appearing within heavens' reach, were already beginning to funnel drapes of liquid along previously unknown hills and valleys of my person; a bullet fired from a distance.

Note:

To whomever était *en charge*
In the last twenty-four
ATTENTION:

Please locate bulletins dated
Yesterday

Small walls, small world.

Being twenty segments younger and, in a rainy state of mind (me without doubting), the presently vacant avenues, presently gathering a plethora of refreshment, would see me skipping and frolicking to dryer ground. In my present state, I watched a perky, carefree individual run through the massacre already evidenced, and enjoyed both the memory and the fresh air. Prior to any of them fancy duds, of course, is the now. It sits on it's throne, beckoning all to bow to its mighty steam-pony, Beauregard, nicknamed Little Beau Boo, for you players of the scorecard.

His time here is so short, by the time you know of it, it's, again, too late. To remember what will make you happy, is not an invitation to ditch life, but take time to enjoy it.

A laugh had to appear after that load and, it did, at an inappropriate fingertip hanging time. The extra boost of chuckling energy, however, did repel me free of the transportable's door, as it closed successfully, with a final click. That's one piece of magic that only occurs here, under these same wet after-storm conditions. The car door closes on it's own and, again

> *I don't want to know*
> *But*
> *It is I cool*
> *There*
> *The title worked its way*
> *Into the story*

My determination ***roger that*** force focused on the only visible dry spot available; inside the next world; while my feet began to shuffle forward, catching the faint rhythm of some memorable tune. Soon, my focus gladly forfeited it's center of attention, the rain, and the world, for a brighter spot.

I don't care about being wet; that would be a luxury; but, the stroll gives one time to center one's self, to forget about life for a moment and, maybe, think about abilities.

The dark lettering, followed by a 'clack', no longer appeared. Paper, strewn with foreign language, was my only friend and, by the looks of it, as stained as it's possessor. Somewhere along the supply line there is the 'Cup of Pita' lying over, being fatally wounded, and, no doubt, pretending to be dead, already. My eyes couldn't break contact with the silent stream of word-forming letters appearing in succession over what used to be my scribbling, on my paper.

I waited for the silence of the dictation to be replaced with any noise having some resemblance to a next breath, which had pulled anchor immediately after the secret screening had begun, and was not going to be back in time to see me faint. I gasped; a cat screamed, two partridges showed up for Savior's Week, my car backfired, a cork sprang free in one of my neighbors bottles, and my panic was a little louder than first thought. My neck chain popped, as my head snapped around without thinking. The new script presented itself in full blackened tribute, before it disintegrated dot by miraculous dot

It takes too long
To answer prayers

I've seen it all before; the evidence, the stenowriter, the paper, the prayers, etc. and etc. The list is long. During the darkness, there were explanations for the hallucinations and having too much of too much would be a signal ignored, offering a living breath to a darkness that was never perceived and, if it wanted to stay around until it became exhausting, that's what it did. It's amazing how having too much will cause excess baggage to appear, at the worst possible times; when the red ticket slaps you in the forehead. Then, there are not only seventeen fronts to defend, with the personal battles, but, thrice as many, with awkward alliances being formed between two former enemies; which is the most awkward evolutionary theory ever presented.

Before my concentration was broken, and the words literally fell away, I had written about a drive that has been performed relentlessly, on four sets of tires, two banjos, and a squeeze tube of medicated gello, for my inflamed little toe. It's been a segment since the darkness left and, in my present situation, and with conditions of life being as they are, it has yet to saunter back.

The darkness, a beast of an alter ego, choked breath out so fiercely no animal, of any kind, can survive it's hate. Instead of having what it most desired, it drove out the angelic for what it deserved but, a greater gift took away the wanting, and filled the abundantly open spaces, still scarred by life's tracks, with a patience and peace never before known

It's a matter of time

Before a wrestling match takes place between you and a visionless reptilian dragon, bent on destroying its host and anyone else who dared enter its lair. Is it the animal *you do realize, we are* within us who refuses to recognize its own behavior and/or adjust the same, even when life, itself, brings its own wrath to bear, in retaliation for unsanctioned transgressions.

We are built to be unhappy, by nature.

To further the argument, I must admit, I am both, a born again Christian, and an evolutionist; believing in the sacrifice made and, 'our greatest of ancestors strolled onto a beach', ideology. If a few of us were to have big webbed feet, the theory would be; We jumped onto a boulder lying near a beach, lying near a tree, hollowed out by a three legged cantaloupe, during the peak of mating season

It's a beach
At least

Being honest with myself, I have to ponder the writings of my Strength, especially where the expulsion of one is concerned. If what I am told is the only truth; in the beginning, the village existed

Do the math

Not one of us is happy all the time because, as animals, we don't have an understanding of the issues within ourselves therefore, we struggle to accept us. Which leads to another quandary; is This All There Is, and, there's never enough time to resolve everything, every problem we have, so we concentrate on the issues surrounding us. They're there. I can see them. It's the cure we all find; to fix them.

Is the couch comfortable?

By the **way**
Mis*ter* **Jacobs**
hypertension *is* ***from*** *aggravation*
I'm **gonna** *write* **you a** *script*
(**GENER**ators begin shutting down)
(A GENTLE WOman's voice plays)
Automated shutdown seq
That's supposed to be three
canines and Jingle Bleeps
(+$&+)
(+$&#!!+)

Have you seen a transportation vessel repair itself? No, because it can't. We can zap a cure on it, right now, because we built it, or, at the least, someone wrote a book about the article's ways and means so, people like me, who are anxious to know it's workings, don't stick an appendage into the ignition sequence generator.

Dwelling into the unknown is a trait, a curiosity, built into all animals, even if we don't have the extravagance of nine lives to bounce back from. Regression and patience are the responses taken to attempt to correct errors of the past. Despite it all, each time I revisit the places I'd rather not, the pictures and videos, once fully accessible, become faded and slightly farther away. Our world, not unlike the universe, itself, expands outwards, until our lives float into a dimly lit abyss, just beyond our reach.

My image reflects back from the mirror across the bar

Hello bar

A hand reaches for the glass balancing itself atop the polished grain. It never matters what the faux crystal contains, it only matters that it does. As long as there's a subtle clink of glass to its contents, the yearning is somewhat soothed, even before its freely exposed liquid graces my lips. That life juice, for me, chilled by the gods of a frozen world, restores hope in a faith lost, and a longing for a time fading away

There or Here
Lies the problem

I motion for another round, as one seventeen nil theremins by, as my eyes watch, while my memory retraces Max's instinctive body, repeating with fluent motion, the actions of a skilled bartender.

He has been here for as long as I, but, my genesis began at zero, as did his for me but, my zero is twenty seven lightyears from any of his. He owns the place, runs the place, and is old enough to hate the place as much as anyone else but, he's still pleasant and present, after what would be considered 'having too much' but, there's better, more obvious things to discuss, now that you brought it up.

Like, the spirits permanently entrenched amongst the ancient architecture surrounding us. They linger, with an audience, who also wait for an infinity of time to pass, and, afraid to inform but, as with any democratic society, there is an admission charge made to our unsolicited friends, the all important 'red ticket', which contains its share of firewater. For myself, being a spell-bound witness to these unsettled souls, for as long as it has been, their presence reaffirms only one thing; if a ghost walks through walls, how can it stand on anything; they're ghosts. Weightless has the same definition now it had back then, when they were.

Are they defying the laws of gravity by merely being or, are they presenting themselves as a projection of reality from another dimension? The debate is moot, because it has been unanimously agreed upon, by the presiding Chamber, Us, that this is a question and subject best left where it resides; in the dark.

If there is, by life's chances, a virgin sitting down to partake of the subtle soothsayers' entertainment fee, the bashful and unknowing are suddenly awakened, causing coin and paper money to be tossed straight towards the heavens, followed by the sound of an angel getting its wings, followed by the splattering of coin landing about. Several times have I been present during these performances but, being accustomed to the show, I only cringe when one pulls up a space beside me. And, actually, the only time I've ever been accused of rolling my eyes, while my creaks and moans rolled with me, is when I'm offered a lapdance.

Max always acknowledges my energetic friend and asks, with a smirk,

"Where'd you get that one!?"

Our unanimous brow raising tells the rest of the story, including, my moving again, when I get my spot back.

Max, as a friend, has spirit, too. It glowed my first step inside the place and with the first words spoken, a friendship had been born. He, along with a couple other members of the Chamber have been witness to my past segment, and to segments prior. They know by my, always meant to be, cordial greetings, and, by my solitude and distance afterwards, that sometimes people just needed to breathe.

My light, unlike Max's, is farther away tonight and just a hint we don't ever say this joint or this dive within these walls it's why the spirits are and among a couple other choice references, those words are at the bottom of the list. Max is married to the bar and, by his own words, can call it what he wants.

Marriage is an odd thing.

He replaces my empty, with a smile and a thank you, which is always sincere. That's what makes the place; his light, his atmosphere. It has to be. There's absolutely nothing to do in here but drink and talk, if both are needed.

The only attempt at bringing in anything amusing and doable is an old video poker machine Max has positioned at the elbow of the bar. Without gambling, it had no hope of success from it's very beginning and, getting the highest score turned out to be less exciting than Mandy, Max's cousin, who, by the way, has dibs on finding the machine a new geographic location, when time appropriate.

She is a jolly drinker, her presence is never unwanted and doubland, her home is beyond the phrase, eclectic. So, the video artwork, once relinquished from its present owner, will fit nicely in whatever corner she already knows it's going in.

Her personal look sets the scale for a response,

as does, on a quadratismal scale, her residence, but, she has been related four times and must have cashed each time, because she works at her favorite hobby, constantly. And, every time she comes in, which is about as often as myself

Can't miss me
From open till boredom

She wears something sparkly, any thing sparkly, as a standard. It can be a new jacket, a hat, or 'just a scarf' but, her presence, and wardrobe is full of the sparklies.

My hand automatically tipped my empty towards its goal

Now serving
Over one trillion triads
To the lucky recluse
Having the lap dance

The barkeep's response is pleasurably immediate *I think they got 'em premixed*

Fingers, with sporadic sensitivities, caressed the condensation clinging to my empty, saying goodbye to it's lifegiving dedication, it's still breathing husk merely, and thoughtlessly, toted away.

When you sit back, entangle your fingers within

your hair, close the eyes, clear your mind, and disappear, is the closest to dying you'll ever be; that is, of course, you're not becoming a participant in the actual fact. I don't know if I did and came back with a new outlook, which, by the way, is freely given and, freely given away; or, I heard what I heard and was conscious enough to know it's sound.

Twenty segments ago, rehab was the only way and through desperation, I had finally gotten the help that was wanted and, abundantly needed, but, you gotta want it. I didn't the first time but, soon after, the second suddenly took over the number one spot, with no resistance

It worked for a while

A helluva long while, in dog years, if you try to fool yourself. If I believe in the science, it's not my fault. It's in the genes, or, maybe a homophone might be suitable, also. That kind of thinking is exactly why my fifth drink in forty-five is about to be ordered.

I already know that the darkness is, or was here. I don't understand why the catch; what kind of bait was used, were the gales hailing out of the east, and is little Johnathon funny, when he's not occupying paper? And, not my strongest category but, when a good, life changing decision hasn't spawned from my intellect in, I don't know how long, there comes a time to be concerned. I think I got tired first, followed shortly by giving up and, that hollow, rattling breath still haunts me

We go on with life
Alone
The way it needs to be

Max leans towards me, as he replaces my old friend for a new one. Picking up multiples of the overflowing canisters in life, tended to generate enough motion for at least my head to lean forward, miming paying attention.

"Somebody told me…", he started, his head quickly, for me, looked both ways.

"…that you're picking" Him, adding another double take. At this, my walls flared up, just in time for the deflection to come but, experience perks his nearly vacant head up and out of the ashes to scold me with eyes looking sharply over dark rimmed glasses.

"You're goin' with the Padres, again this season!?" The accent being held on the sentence, which, as expected, brought prodigal boos from the small, nonpartisan gathering of about six, minus Mandy, myself, and Max.

When there were no interesting conversations around, I could yell out, "Fault a guy for being dedicated" to something other than himself but, I never did. The joke was funny, and we had no idea there was such a lack of support for my team again, this segment. It was quite the cackle last season, also, before we swept, in four straight, with me marveling, too. My bet was on five three.

With the front door opening, a small bell floated across air waves, echoing off wood and glass alike, adding to it's indigenous orchestration. I looked at my phone; yes, it was Mandy time, guaranteed by the family's greeting.

Never having been much of a rubbernecker, I returned to the image in front of me, and thought of something I really didn't care about. It was also time for deep thoughts to lay low; they would fracture in a few minutes with Mandy's greetings, and, sometimes, the slightest little thought might bring back important information.

"Hi, Dale"

Mandy's voice was squeaky, at best, and, honestly, became more tolerable with each round, but, my body and my greeting happily turned her way, automatically accepting the hug offered.

"You doing ok?" She always asked, and always meant it.

If you looked around, you might think that we're just a bunch of old and worn out drunks sitting around watching the world go by. The irony of that observation would be the least of our problems. But, I've never taken a poll, but that's about the extent of our issue, on a day to day timeframe. Waiting.

On weekends, Max has a "real" bartender take over command of the buoyancy tantalizer. It's noisier, prices are stable, and it's behind door number two. Max, for himself, doesn't accept tipping but, he's 'only helping out a few college kids, who couldn't get the extra shift down the road. Hint hint.'

"They're all good kids" he says, with eternally pessimistic optimism. Life is like a box of newly refurbished waffle makers, and no one has ever really thunk that planting gobbledegook inside is all that's needed to grow the pitted discs, have they? An entire molecular culmination must take place, with first aligning the littlest in the middle and surrounding them with, no, wait, that's pancakes

My bad

Having an extra body to hang with, as long as they do my job, gives Max an opportunity to carouse with his clienteli, but it's not so easy to pick him out of a lineup, after he steps out of one reality and into another. He is a business man and takes advantage of the small increase in sales to entertain his new and old guests with laughable conversations throughout the nite; giving them the release they need. After sunset, it's a don't ask, don't tell, don't look, maybe no one will notice policy; especially, on the weekends.

Mandy had released our intimacy and had moved her attention to my right, bypassing my next door friend and, what many patients of our establishment would consider an outhouse-building-of-a-good-time but, he was ignored

I think

And, by his expression, didn't care.

Mandy followed her own routine on the runway, like anyone else, stopping by each sitting Chamber member to wish them a good day, without an air of relative affluence. She is a sweet human and beats me hands down.

Max and her could actually pass as siblings, each having the same taste in, and, the astounding ability to discover the oddest, most fitting decor. Mandy's self proclaimed destiny is to keep her cousin's establishment up with the times. Whichever historical publication is being referenced to come to the conclusion that times is a nominal word and, well, talent is talent.

She'll browse an outlet, find something interesting enough to dazzle her juices, then, continue searching until she has ‹the full set›. The set doesn›t necessarily mean anything is in its original all in one packaging, it falls together in scattered remnants and is then designed into their perfect positions somewhere on the walls, the ceiling, or the customers, themselves, and, presto, Art's Max Exhibit has a new masterpiece.

What we haven't figured out yet is if our fellow spirits have accepted Mandy's work, or even notices it. And, always me, being suspicious of what can't be touched, there could be a renovation plan secretly in the works from our occupier.

It is curious. I would trust a spirit to be up to something; him not having the ability to grasp an idea, much less

And yes
Saw the flick
Don't buy it

Pool, and kids, like we wish our overstaying guests would do, went away a while ago, I had realized, after thinking about the Mod Squad's hangout, a few blocks away. A number of the crowd, including the weekend warriors seemed to like Max's place, and would drop by on occasion but, most were like us and didn't get by there that often.

Mandy's hand brushed across my back, as her

first class round trip jet airliner entered into its final approach, normally four stools down from mine. Neither stool, at my right and left, has been worn by, what you call, buttocks

Gravity yes
Apparently

The tops of stools look like deflated toadstools, with the seats caved in. No one, with me tagging along for another affirming vote, dared touch, or move them. Company, on crowded nights, had no place to sit, with there being no stools. On not so busy nights, company was steered clear, us fearing the illegal aliens would retaliate and do nasty things to the unsuspecting, and what would be, no doubt, an unwilling participant.

I live my life like I'm riding sidesaddle in the masquerade to end all. Alone, with not even a horse. Which is why I like the place as much as I do. I was a drunk before I made my run in the Series, and I was a drunk before the first book. In Max's Exhibit and Art Show, I was merely a concerned citizen, who needed a drink. That's all my identification papers directed me to do and, most times, I couldn't get the thing out of the wallet, anyways.

I know everyone here abouts knows, but there's never been a conversation regarding what I do for a living. For all who knows, for all they care, I'm retired. There was this one fella' who's better half must have had lying around his house, the one book of mine, not displaying a picture of me. He knew me but not my work. I did the math and talked him through his consumption of the appropriate grounding lubricants, before we shook, and said our farewells. I got to know him better than he me and, hopefully, he doesn't realize my evasion when he announces to his crowd that he bought a drink for somebody famous.

"Who was it?"
"I have no idea."

Max would always refund the person's money, without them knowing, and put the beverage on my tab. I appreciated their gestures of hospitality and the need for a story but, for me, I knew nothing was deserved. It's something to get used to, this crucifixion of mine. But, again, I like the place. It's solitary confinement, at it's best.

A clattering of newly washed dishes broke my silence, and again, looking around, there was nothing to do here. Plus, it was getting blurry outside, which signaled my authoriti to make it my last call

Houston

My matinee, usually full color and in HD, spoke as loudly as it needed, being amongst relatives, and all. The passing point had been reached and was exactly where it wanted to be, probably, minus one. If a feeling of victorious satisfaction had swept over me upon this realization, another round would have been welcomed but, a sense of loathing could have come just as easily. I am the insatiable one.

Numbness was a benefit invited and to be joyously celebrated, along with silence, which, all too often, fades away. There is no joy when the beast is near but, I figure me and Slim here can last eight seconds a piece on the ratly stallion, maybe wear him done a bit.

My glazed but enlightened glaze rode it's coaster to my half-full glass, or was it half-empty, it's hard to tell. It then continued it's bouncy ways to the exhausted pack of smokes lying alongside the wet ring, left by the glass. The crumpled packaging looked as if it had seen better days, and was waiting for the eight-count to conclude, so it could tuck its tail and find a new career. A wiggle came, as the squares' only response

Good girl

I thought it peculiar, too.

My body, eased off it's throne, in all different directions, looking, I imagined, like a squid on glass, with it's walleye expression, both frozen and amused, and anticipating a full frontal on the next passing ship. My digits came to the ready and tested for potentials, while my feet stretched another two inches to reach the solid floor beneath them. A faint gaseous sound released itself with my full risen weight but, being a gentleman, and a squeaking board to everyone else, I excused myself, quietly.

In one practiced swoop, the distance between the door, my hand, and a world unworthy of sobriety lessened with each farewell pat on the back and offered goodbye. With another child receiving enlightenment, and with these ones outside never giving up, I hoped I could remember all this in the morning.

Chapter Two

...might Need An Editor!

Rain was good, my belief conversed, adding that the bombers had withdrawn slightly from their assault and, maybe, chose to also plod to higher ground; they must be missing Mr. T and his motivational words.

Storms followed pleasantries, followed intense catastrophes, followed fiery heat; it is the mode of nature. It was the targeting and the piercing leaves now, just following the storms, which become the immediate danger.

The most disturbing issue is trees haven't been around these gardens for triple set three segments, or so, and no one has been able to travel far enough outside and into the zone to discover the origin of these organic missiles, nor have many cared to attempt the research..

I shuffled, as quickly as possible, while the ringing door behind me closed on itself; no magic, just good ventilation. My luck, after all, was best folded, and not pressed, even if it was my day. My bar-hugger buddy friend, who also folded upon exit, if that's possible, never made it this far. His song and dance was a sham and, come to think of it. Unable to shut it down, an all systems alert split the uprights in a gravitationally challenged dodge ball game, and again, the follower of that yellow line is ignoring all coordination and straight line status reports; if only I could connect one to the other; in favor of stealthily frolicking and sliding and attempting to reconnect telemetry to the rhythm depot found previous, which, under the present terms, would be more difficult than it sounded.

So, you're playing a foolish game, matching a trio of items, not suitable for digestion, none. Foolish is a word that might be described in verse but, it's true meaning is only thought, or spoken, and this game presents you with a predicament.

There are two items left to be zapped, but they are on separate and opposing tracks, with only two shots remaining in a magazine of thirty-five rounds. The shot would be impossible, save a completely lucky one, bouncing into contact with every other bouncy face involved in this legalized disaster, as your attention turns elsewhere, or, take the shot and trip on it's trip; your choice.

It's the first time this diagram has been the challenge, and passing through the magazine would be simple, attempting, as you do, to get lucky punk, but you have buffs. And, unlike golfing, these have been given at little, or no cost to you.

And, I have failed to understand my wanting to set the volume level of my audiophonic device to an odd number except, and when, that number is thirteen. As rules state:

It is now acceptable *legislation changed it from not* to place volume magnitudes to either side of this inbred number. The complete absurdity, by following instructions sets forth the scenario where power will be obtained by both the blue tiles, and the even tiles, who never give it back, ever. If hesitation or distraction encumbers too long; hovering will cause power adjustments, and like a bell and an angel, a click will be heard, when time has changed. Many times, have I tempted fate, pushing harder in each instance, counting every microsecond as my last, but, never really being that mindless.

My hands, reaching as high as their adjoining members would allow, politely wave to the uppermost layers of the nite's peaceful sky. It's lunar orbital, a bit wobbly, at times, stands steadfast at her post, but, what will begin in seven slip two segments, of whom's biological baby sister recently passed through us, will create another ground zero in a world grown weary. Our alternate ego, on the south side of a global nowhere, now dodges their matinee allday performance of the monstrosity.

As cyclical as it is, and as unyielding as it's determined fangs are, it's a wonder why anyone remains and is continuing to live in it's path, without excavating hundreds of decibels deep, and dodging its influence, as many before have. But, there are times when a populist vote doesn't attain the results we seek. The mouthbreathers, seen on the walkways, in the square, and at the malls, decided their own fate, and having accepted nature's prowess and fury as the punctuated conclusion to a welcomed end. We live where we do, because of where we live. With a vindictive world propagating disaster, depleting multiple sections of both land and mortal alike, our numbers and the availability of venues suitable enough to survive, dwindle, creating fruitless dumbbell societies destined to extinction. A resilient shield repairs what it can, and lives the best it can but, having no expectations for a better future, beyond the next day and green grass, will alter a man's resolve.

A thought, bouncing somewhere betwixt the frontal lobes *my eyes move so I know they're working* hit the afterburner and was

(**UPBEAT JAZZ**aFonic**S** plays)

Let's welcome

Dave den Cancoon

To the show everyone

(**A CROWD** roars' it's cheers)

Yes

Yes sir

(**CHE**ers)

Thank you

Uh

You all

Listen

Yeah man

Certainly

What's going on there big D little d

I got this email

Yeah man😵

About the biosystemic emaluations

Entitled

Preshow Guest Evaluation

Yeah man😕

They call it

The page

Hey

Cool man

Yeah uh Mister DDC

You can omg all you
Oh yeah man
Easy Dave
Those evals are sent
Oh man yeah
Some guests gettum twice a week
(**UPBEAT JAZZ**aFonic**S** plays)
We'd like the thank
Our accredited mania
(**A HOOPALIS**hciou**S** theme plays)
MOCOA CHOLA
(**IN TRIPL**icate, voices sing)
MADE IN BUTTER
(**UPBEAT JAZZAF**onic**S** plays)
We'll be back
Next Hunsday
With our special meteoric
Supah Dupah
Kooleoo Mieco Supbloman
Goodnight everybody

Trains of thought, ample in my youth and presently skipped across synapses after any other fancy wordesis, constantly, making me feel like I'm being shagged in the fastest pitching and batting duel to ever be recorded into the history of games, which by the way are now three cube two of Pegs O'licious Gravies in length, to center is five hunddred Shhh, and

> *The tropics*
> *Are so nice*
> *This time of year*

My exhaustion took a breath, clearing the world for a moment, while joining another discussion on what an amazing product we humans are. Our mental capabilities and a state of consciousness, evidently, has been around for a while but, our instinct to buy-here-sell-here is as ingrained in us as our favorite color, which can only be one actually; with no combinations of differing hues or luminosities

> *Can I get my first choice*

So funny *you'll lose a stripe over it stop it remember the calculating structure of our intellectual abilities,* and, without fail, getting us anywhere

> *Imagine*
> *Anywhere*
> *But here*

Although, segway, our wanting to survive, and at the minimal, a short excursion near the edge of the zone, which is excursely made shorter still, by faulty superimposed apparatus mechanisms, causing us to what *wait for it* develop better survival functions *way to go thought I'd lost ya*

Any ideas

A slide flies by, signaling, we should have thought more about the overpriced extended warranty program and following the slidden headline is a double feature sequel beginning with a streaming of the outer space wannago group, in a thousand years:

The most technologically advanced rocket to ever be designed sits idly, sleeping in a cradle to it's form; the launch sequence paused by unknown and offsite issues. Within twenty four clicks, the born again missile, with it's massive thrusting power, will shoot a manned rocket into a spacial thirty-five segment round trip journey.

It's mission; to get back. And, upon its return and within its descending arc towards the planet, a hook and arm gills the vessel, drawing it back downwards, aiding in the remainder of its final voyage. There have been only seventeen or eighteen lost, due to a slippery hook not being properly maintained.

But, the autopsy of the lifeless passengers, who will remain inside the locked ship for another twenty-four, will begin promptly, thereafter. The constructors of the ventilation conduits still don't know what they're missing.

The greatest quote, made by someone who I knew, knew stuff

"Oh yeah. We can get 'cha there."

Man's search continues for; with what amount of our time will it take us to evolve, and will it happen in our lifetime no one knows I showed you and, will we become more than our cups can bear.

The image looking back at me, both grey and weathered, and, tired and alone, has plotted many courses, both tangible and imagined, in his search for a grail, whose fantastic existence is better left in the editorial columns of, *Cups and Saucers Weekly,* and I'm getting nowhere.

Maybe happiness has passed me by this round; my pleading condition, a future; gave 'er a try, an attitude, which is laced with arsenic, and heavenly bodies falling from the sky; and, accepted, if I am. If anything is left in the heavenly's when the greatest meteor shower, of all time, has nothing else to drop. The line, no longer lines, to any heavenly host is very short; they have surpassed expediting on a grandiose scale. Or, maybe their napping intelligence was awakened, when one their twinkling stepping stones swept by their bedroom window, too. And, not really taking it seriously before, there is no clue, at all, as to what might be my next chance. Meaning, if this newly installed gadget; offered on the black market by them upstairs; is at all time specific, the transatomic stenograph's numeric configuration will be set to, 'over there'

Hey
Whaddahyooz want
An orbitchuwary

Did you know that, while in a moving object, with no wind without, with your face turned to it, it becomes its own directional gauge. The wind, never existing, will obey commands, and never change direction. Put me down for a few, and go find some wind but, before you go, it would lead to the question of, if no wind, no turbulence? That's as easy as answering the question, no life, no death

If you get a call
Asking for your support
In conquering death
Pass

We can't keep allowing ourselves to be us. Our turbulence is ending in a merry dance to no timeout land. No miracle trance, or leader, is going to pull us out of the nose dive we are in. And, if one does rise, trusting it for a promised land, with the aroma of hate surrounding it, sheeletle will not be a choice

We are blaming the mightiest
for all our problems

And yes, I asked

Why the old
Then the New
One filled with love
The other with blue
This is what you get
When we are left with you

When it has little to do with anything but, us. It has something to do with the other but, by giving us a freedom no one else will ever give, in any lifetime, and our willingness to trade this gift for a better set of playing tags; it is the created and the evolved in conflict, with bigger sticks than we could ever fathom. And, why is it that, on this phone, when I'm deleting large open spaces *don't ask why probably yesterday's notes* and, doing it one line at a time, does text at the bottom of my screen rise? The animal in us, created and evolved, thirsts for

72

knowledge but, by utilizing the comprehension level of a gnat; we forget too conveniently.

My gravitationally challenged steps, between illusion and reality, are few. It's a small place, my home; outfitted to the minimal, with living conditions more than adequately furnished; the steno and paper was also an anonymous gift. Comfort is described in so many ways, shapes, and forms. Among those still breathing, as many have categories of choices to consider, to determine an acceptable outcome for themselves. Some recame for down under, others went farther away to do the same, still others went that away and didn't care. Several were last seen going into the storm and couldn't be stopped.

Once a pin falls into place, in the lock of life, keying the gross remaining didn't look that difficult on paper. But, that's with locks physical in nature, and, securely bolting assets residual to a life lived and not the quagmire of rationales splattering across my Pinnacle, at any given moment.

With a nagging, phantom pain *one who's electricals must be short circuiting* irritating by movement, my attention returned to the partial page of letters resting in their tree of life; curiosity made me glance towards the bottom. The very active interactive nerve ending paced my intentions, making me look like one of those boppers *what did they call them* the Skeetles. That's what it was and, presently, my grunts had the beat down flat.

"Nothing new here, Spike!" came my rhythmic answer, in an attempted and somewhat confused mimicking of a Tres Bien Amigos' treasure

Well

There was an hypothesis' the other year ago, theorizing the evolution of animals and what these scientifically challenged 'noids decided the showcased animals would look like, when they evolved, again?

That's all it took

I don't care
If an octopus
Struts down Vakas Boulevard
Wearing one leg and a boot

I was surprised, and am ashamed to repeat the headline:

Walking in Memphis

During the twelve nine World's Fair.

How much evolution is it going to take, to get us to that something that is beyond us? And, we're not talking about the biopod operating Dwarf fish, recently ticketed for obnoxiously utilizing roadways. I didn't think road rage could be redefined

Will brains
And Or
Money win

My wager is on the money, and the fortunate few, vending each other *because I can* for next to nothing. The jockeys, in this montagemic extravaganza, with crop in hand and riding fierce and steaming yearlings, smite the perceived ne'erdowells into compliance but

Actually
That's very exaggerated
Excuse the drama

They're the tiniest, most harmless little things, riding on the back of fleas. If you've ever been in a situation where there are an amount of fleas, you know how noisy it is. And, they can't help what they're riding, it's the only thing their saddles will fit, and the biting is just flavor comparison testing, ordered by your local veterinarian.

In an evolved future, powered by sextuplet E batteries, our remains are discovered, and being broadcast live to the solar system. A lone figure is unveiled in the solarcast, sitting comfortably in a bentwood rocker. His mummified hand holds a mysteriously cavernous and crystallic object, partially full, for those curious

What is to become of us

Our ancestral tree meets at least one fork during its quest, says hello, takes a *god knows where* turn and ends up here. For all we know, we are the sixteen balls, the stick is another of the, I don't want to know 'Rally', and, the players are us *and again not a word*

Rerack please
Not again
I'm further out this time
How 'bout some cheese
For the li'l fella'

I must have gone into a deeper sleep than was led to believe, and slept through the eighteen hundreds. Who's wanting to be right in this catastrophe waiting to happen

You
Go to line two

It is a fair question because, obviously, we done good, so far. Like the odds and evens, the blues and the reds, we gather behind an alignment of beliefs, to apply our logic to the next, so they'll be okayed, too.

Let's stop the transcendintunal posturing, and let the battle cry's ring diagonally across the wires of constipation, like they always do

Roll Out

I don't believe, in my most dedicated corpuscle, that I'd do no worse than what has been offered us thus far, with exception *and no i will not say that loud enough for you to hear me* It's up to you to take advantage of whatever it is that is in your path and, to tame it. Unless, of course, you've fallen out of favor with whomever is talking, or, a video poker machine is within your reach, your destiny is scribed. Whichever path you choose will be yours chosen; feel it's tentacles, hear it's beckoning call, you, lost in it's grace, mesmerized by the feeling of belonging, will kick the tires at your own risk

Thank you

If you could have seen the drive in tonight, minus light refraction and moisture, you'd have seen another spectacular site, containing all the raybonic colors. It is odd, how the weather is acting but, I wouldn't trade a beautiful sunset for anything known to man.

My head, thankfully remaining dry, sticks itself out and into what must be a torn and tattered air pocket above. The storms, lately, have become even more severe; each new showerly wind rips away what remains of our outer protective layers. It's penetrating rays have crippled industry and perforated any shield known to us, or manufactured by us. Each day the world breathes, each nite Apollo syphons.

The coldness, to whichever persistent digits remained, brought a shiver to my hand as it caressed the fruity, umbrella containing concoction bestowed upon me. The newest tender, Lavine; she's as sweet as a cherry pie; had asked if a trip on the wild side would be appropriate, today. Me, not knowing where this conversation would eventually end

Did she just

I hesitantly said, sure.

Far be it from me to anticipate the wild would consist of a sweet aftertaste and a parasol. The tingle, again, of the first microbial drop of sustenance touching buds, still refreshed a rotting soul, and, of course, the sunshade was left in the glass. It felt sacrilegious not to have it's ancient presence purty up the place. Max had stashed them under the commode after the last beach week

> *I'm afraid to ask*
> *But what was being looked for*
> *When the discovery was made*

And, yes, it's still my day and I'll genetically alter anyone who calls it, Muoorsmay. Peace has been offered, umbrellically, and my interest peaked enough to take on the challenge that, apparently, no one else would take, or, they all did and are getting there sooner than me. It would be rude not to accept an offering, in good faith, from a stranger, who opens my bottles. I'm a trusting person, when the commissary board pieces are laid out as they are.

Max was down the trail in a talker but, not wanting to be impolite, he came by to say his welcomes, and to verify that I'm not performing a frontal lobotomy with the blowfish that just didn't get it.

He smiled.

"I know what you're thinkin'"

A spotlight turned on, nailing me between my eyes, with me knowing he had no idea

and why exactly are those three marks just hanging there. That's not normal.

He grabbed my forearm, with a friend's shake and

retraced his steps to continue whichever debate du jour
had polished its hooves for the trip. He knew as well as
I, the reinforcement personnel attached to units *and hey
that request was put in yesterday* that we'd be here for
a few. Me knowing a glint of light, randomly selected
in the lottery of beams will, no doubt, send me into a
downwardly funneling pit, that was either being worked
on or *pardon our progress* are closed for renovations

Yessindeedee
My time was good

Take a Lippy's lighter, for instance, where one was
found, over two hundred segments ago; long before
the almighty weasel appeared but, suggestively and
ironically, under the original and virgin ground zero.

The specimen *I know what you're thinking* was sent
for processing (**BLACK MAR**ket *prices plays*) along
with other debris, and the Lippy's decal, flint, wick and
body were all intact, and flawless.

After being cleaned, and with fluid applied, it lit;
after three flint replicas were manufactured, and later,
an operations manual located. Which can be understood,
never having owned one, myself, but, partaking, on
occasion, of the other habit, causing a need for the lost
one. It would also fill a vacancy in my collection, and

give me an interesting toy to play with. Their aroma can give the essence of an aphrodisiac

Sorry
Not the word
I was looking for
But
You get the idea

Without thinking any further, decide if my stripes should be reinstated, based on that argument. It's up to you. Thanks a bunch!

Max also knew better than to wake me before my receptors were prepared for outside stimuli; I have to be conscious. It sounds worse than it is. Quirky people staycation in the place and Max has a knack with quirky people, he's a natural. The length of friendship, and frequency of participation in Chamber rituals, has no memory of time spent, when time only means lack.

My greatest appreciation for him, and anyone, is, when you save an angel, before entry or, after clocking out, your business, while taking up space within these hallowed walls is never repeated. Ever. The price, meant because of me, but appreciated by all, was losing a piece of hide along the posterior regions. I've never witnessed it but, rumor is, it hurts. There's a quirk for everyone and we all slip on our pedestals, from time to time but, there are no excuses for betraying a confidence.

Max liked hiding, too. He got it.

If a hovercraft were to appear in the square, and all occupants disembarking wore militaristic uniforms supporting the banner of Sleknic, and, with whom, strolled a darkened filine, so dark it consumed ambient light

Not a peep

"You are a bit of a dull boy. Aren't 'cha, mate?"

Max's poking was a more cordial way of tapping a person on the shoulder, and with my glass replaced and elated, he chuckled, and quickly returned to the rodeo, dropping the empty into a sink tub full of soapy water. Knowing Max, the session was about business; if it's about commerce, he'll sit down and chat but, to be honest, the b'sing, once freely available, and drawn at a moments notice, is overshadowed by future, unseen events

No matter what be you've heard
And

Forecasting storms, by visual means, is made more difficult, unless the witnessing is accomplished personally and relayed to *whatever* the masses by spotted shortwave. The overseers, as a whole, have been pardoned from blame for wanting to remain sheltered. The only volunteer, who has braved the rapids, by having her jersey retired shortly after she left no forwarding address and I couldn't remember my name.

With the functionality and telescopics of Kysinski's radar predicting us as a stormpath, us being annihilated in a fortnite eight past, our intuitiveness to wrangle a last deal, instead of enjoying the beauty while we can.

A person can be talented enough to repaint the smile on D'tangelo's masterpiece but, when *she* walks down Vagas Boulevard, I will then believe a piece of canvas, or a boot, means anything.

I'm thinking of a go at the video poker era but, thinking of the recycling of nomadic sequences, the thought quickly passes.

Look into glass, he says.

It'll be good for you, he says.

The reflection staring back at me, no different from any at home *poor old greying siamese twin guy* a simple fact. The same pattern is used in the construction of every mirror, in every world, ever made. Ever ever. And, they, without heed, increase the price to an exorbitant amount, knowing you're going to buy it and, preferably, by the pair.

It's you!

Of course it is. I love it!

Usually, you are obligated to buy one for it to reflect mostly on you but, yours can be borrowed, too. Travel elsewhere, where there are no mirrors or reflections; you will only see, when you don't. The difference in two, when divided, arguing over slush funds, proven by the first, dominated by desperate egos never wrong and, objected to by local politicians.

"This ain't looking good. At all!" says the yocal

Oh

Here's the info

On the Wheel that was promised

It's a holographic ring of mirrors, forty six centimeters tall, and revolving in light generated from within itself. It's mobility, ups and downs, is made possible by a downloadable software special, Frisky Pack A, which is, of course, made possible, after verified purchase of said system

wwx.seeyourselfcsyouare.exe

The spinning was the hook for me, and why that was, at the time of purchase, I'll never know *makes me dizzy* other than it being a neat idea and, I'm not the type who needs certain things to make my agony unbearable. The gadget is popular over the spectrum, with its customized heights and diameters. Width of the mirrored panels can be adjusted a little, but it's best to leave that to the experts; they read your short designer survey. And, from your choices, they will splice together an image of you, it being a telekinetically controlled AI module

Did I say revolving
Already

One day, while in bladder control mode, id est, rushing, as fast as a physical being can; and while floodgates creak open

WHICH
sorry for the yelling
it helps
WAS ALSO A COMPLAINT

Relayed through the proper channels, but, since bedlam has been locked down, following the 'Epidemic of the Flesh', ironically named for its flesh eating skills; the squeamish politios upstairs have even isolated me to my room, where all my stuff is

They had named it
Sorry
I told you that

There have been no overnight passes issued for my crews in weeks, and they'll withdraw themselves from service before a summer's eve, if not reinforced

Them
Not capable of pushing
Much longer

But, in all your dreams, the lighting being the most seductive, I realized my new toy had arrived. I'll not tell you the added story of me not having a night light, and, why I really don't care to have the cadillac of their ship.

For this module, I just got the basics, for which they supplied an extra two blades *be sure to make the upgrades*

It took hours to learn how to use the thing, because thinking, in its essence, is not exactly what basic nucleic reproduction is designed to do, but through advances, and a transfer to a bedding site, my most favorite glowing aura radiated, filling my small toiletry with a pleasantry never before felt. But, ain't there always, it is subscribed to one location, making it pricier, in scale, to other produced models. That is, if you're into that sort of thing, and it matters. The unit's imagery can go through walls, so furniture placement is not an issue, and, in my younger days, the full upgrade might have been attractive, again, in my younger days.

It is designed from you, for you, so, after a few, the thinking process, wobbly at first, was deduced. And, getting it off the ceiling, where it was delivered, in itself, was another feat I do not wish to partake of, again. That's the first challenge; the second is specific connection, made to fine tune syncing, making it possible to where a mind be not cluttered with unneeded processes.

Once syncing is complete, my human favorites, listed on my survey; color, foods, my dream date choice, and/or my significant other's choices, the usual; and my favorites, as designed by my uploaded nucleic blueprint, made available for transmission from our friends at GAP; after permissions were granted *ho hum* which released a pod, to connect to another, both traveling in a tube, created by a telekinetically talented artificial intelligence generator.

This was covered in the fine print, before sale, but it didn't mention to be sure and check box romeo

You'll see why

The craving for an aspirin, or six, became overwhelming. The flash of the reddish coloured laser, fired a few seconds ago, finally and mercifully dimmed it's selfishly imposed spots. It always happens that way; one foot is placed in front of the other, actually getting me over there but, a flash of light tripping, at once, a series of randomly selected internal circuits causing a flood of paraphernalia to swoosh by *makes Jake a dull host* makes lore become real, on a random basis. Or, it could be me, or, I, or my consciousness searching for the answers it seeks but, trains connect to conserve fossils, auras of darkened red populate the pathways, and children pay for us.

I used to think and walk at the same time, like there was a choice back then, and life's discrepancies would pummel from the eaves, in grand style, flying their little bitty biplanes, buzzing around until it was time to make a dump. I like the translucent shell, myself. It's upgraded to the hilt and quiet, and incredibly cheap. Listen, if you wanna drive yourself crazy, at least make the upgrades. Send me a copy of your solar spheres, for postage, and I'll return you a secret.

Fortunately, the discovery was made, as to the effects of translucent refraction and, the near consequences because of its effects: when it moved but wasn't there.

", and then, David started running,"

Max was some kinda guy. Here he was, pretending to have a conversation, gestures and all, with a guy elsewhere. I downed my proportioned frostbite in time to crack a smile, and politely grab my next; downing it before it's eddy had ceased.

"You believe that", he concluded, with more decibels, peering, making sure I was returning from a good place, as he slid another fountain my way.

My glass tipped to the affirmative, thankful for a friend's ability to talk a person off a ledge, in the middle of a storm. We talked about the sweats once, both agreeing to the phrase's contradictions; it's below fifty and not much warmer on my inside and I'm soaking wet, while the outside atmosphere erupted into one of those nasty ones, when only the angels and the demons brave conditions for the sole purpose of waging war.

Max leans close.

"Davy said one picked up a napkin back near the cooler," His delivery was to the point. "...and threw it." I nodded, remembering the holy crap mode earlier, but using a completely different fornicational expression.

It just got interesting.

I'm still not a rubbernecker for anything that's not meant to be my business, so a roll of the dice could be used to guess where my everything behind the back door would be placed. My only interest in specific proximities is the closeness of my next chaser, in relation to what is being discussed.

A few, who still frequented the place, know about them, the presence, and them, only because of the red ticket. They, for all any of us know, are the Chamber.

We call it that, only because of what we felt when a black cloud voted itself guardian on high; a legislative act made unlawful under stationary guidance, by the way. Nobody can ever get a word out of misty's twigs but, seeing what became the cloud above us did sway our vote so much, you might have thought we had a choice in the matter. They've been quiet since, unless you want to count the noise and here we go

Thanks Bob
Our souls have wrestled with
Enough conversations to understand
The word
No

Bob's in command of one of unititled reinforcement garrisons filling in for a troop on holiday, and I'm thinking the missing notes are in someone's overniter.

They demand us to list ingredients on products the contented item possesses. We can decide whether it is good for us, by saying

I did what when

There is no list describing taxes already paid on items we purchase, but, said *Notice of Information* can easily be placed in a pack, or sticker labeled to the bottle.

It's the force fed propaganda we are plastered with, to sway our vote *for a better cause* that continues the strife we, who want to live, live in

Yes

SYMFPHADWIRFAQ

The only news I hear is in here, but doing research brings many stories, catching the attention of whom they are intended, and passing my causeways of interest, from time to time.

The one job I would not enjoy is, as a reporter

Single tense
This is not an opinion
An observation

There are, and have been a few persons who are talented at their work, and being good helps when, and, if there were no announcer, or would we understand the natural sound of the recorded item

Yes
We are not doing
Chapter 3

Of
Let Alone Provider
This evening

Or, our lack of access to certain places, who are beyond our reach, or, having to be in two places at once, are needs' they fill in our life. Witchery; and if I might find the mysteriously *delete my account* button and go away after writing this but

Man
I'm thinking
Lost it
Dagnabbit

If you're so into something, your health and longevity suffer because of its location

I Want It Here
Did you hear me
Here

Move there, with my blessing.

Many new, potential patrons stop by, from all points, and from many directions, to test the squeaks in the floors and measure the layers of dust on the linens, looking for a new place to survive the temperatures, but seldom, do any reappear. Those who do are only here confirming sober, what they thought they saw sheets ago. They too, having fulfilled their oathly duties to whatever group they belonged and, gaining a posh badge for the sacrifice made, are soon long gone. Atmosphere means little to those less fortunate

Me thinks me ready

Well, I came, I saw everything except video poker *didn't even try.* With another Quantum physics question being asked at halftime, I needed to be alert, with processes at the ready and, did not need to be dealing with small numeric sequences when it occurs to me that I'd be as comfortable with partial consciousness *check!* and weekends off but, aren't things just weird. All day has passed without the deadliest trap ever concocted by my fellow man, becoming a subject; an item freely available to smite anyone in it's path.

Any other item, with it's non-discriminatory power to take, ceases to exist and is soon offered to the designers who willingly, with protoplasm salivating from their pores, receive ill gotten gains for the sole purpose of changing its colour's distribution, for redistribution on a galactic scale. It takes away us, and they don't care, unless an interceder reprograms comprehensive workflow charts, sending excess flows to our neighboring fields, who think it's delicious.

Why do you think it can't be stopped; free, lawful Killing? The little green people are not beyond us

We do not see them
They are here
Red eyes
Expressionless faces
Floaty things
In various scales and dynamics
Sound familiar

The Politio's call it *check* Haloes Eve, a celebraic entertainment jamboree *system is a go* during which time Uranus passes the Hycotumus test, the Traloqueal Gambit. And, it winks

You can see them
Everywhere
Hovering over the masses
Peddling their goods
And counting

It's agonizing, death.

I can't speak the word, without being offered something from it's ovens. I can't speak the word against another, without fearing my own demise by the blue haired punk rock group strolling through the gardens, picking allergy free dandelions.

It's a choice to *cue talent*

On TickTalk Live

We have with us

Doctor

Gaylord Infumperry

Welcome Doctor

Thank you

Doctor

Yes

In Kykinski's theorem

Yes

It evaluates

Yes

Atmospheric conditions

By comparing the two

The two too often colliding with

Yes

The ancient Hypoxy's theorem of

Predatory Nucleonics

How would you explain

Yes

Under general conditions

Uh huh

Neonuclar act vity takes place in random
scales throughout our cranium

Uh huh

but mostly within the subdural quarters

Uh huh

Kykinski was a fore-sighted man

Yes

His genius is proven

By his theory of

Participatory Extraction

Participatory extraction

Why yes

Uh huh

The analogs of consistency

Recommend

For every ounce of energy

You try to

Consume during flight

Uh huh

I take offense at *your attitude*

(+&$#!+)

Silence, with only a ringing in the ears, stood steady;
the higher pitched returned first, followed by the lesser
sounds. There was no tunnel here, only a lens' aperture

weakly sliding open; the world presenting itself in both light and sound.

I looked for my coat before realizing the sunny day, and allowed my feet to lead their way through the crowd of one *better not fall I don't think I can catch you this time* and Max, who was double checking my condition and ability to catch myself

Roger that
On my way

I two finger saluted, and nicely.

My lubricated comrades put down what they were reading, the eletricicle components tickled, and, all was Mary with my world. It was an 'all systems kinda hanging out havin a thing and knew it's way to the door, kinda at-ti-tude' but, nicely.

I grunted, with a final wave, as a brush of air came from above me; the environmental stabilizer, presenting fresh movement, whether in or out; and me wondering when that was installed. Although, the pleasantly antagonistic burst of its rush came as two units, when whomever wore a skirt and whomever.

Loving the country is, loving the countryside *used pork is not worth bailing hay i just adore a tramp's house view darling I love you but give me the fatal news* and, with that, a freshness fills the senses, beyond imagination

Watch my pitch

Feet in raw dirt. Non-protective clothing striding along in molecular tandem. A comforting symphonic orchestra, presented by nature's own, drowning out preconceived ideals. Or, the slushing of boots, with flakes as large as pennies floating softly, as the discovery is made of the snow's depth, in relation to the height of the new boots. The welcoming of peace is always silent, when it weighs nothing, after all. Unlike other gadgets, freely available for a sum, in the market across the byway, it works well in frigid temperatures; not as well, sometimes, but, how much company does one need to relax by the fire

My car for a kingdom

Which was now parked beside a larger than thick stick, depending on your visual fortitude; it has girth. It also lay in a spot it hadn't possessed previously, during my landing amid these same coordinates. It was ten micros away from my carpet

That won't help a thing

Sobriety arrived, at the challenge of transposing old world math into modern nomenclature and, having to take a second look, to see whether the unopposed is possible, is a conversation that may appear later, after the science quiz, but, when weapons fall in battle they transform into what the natives believe are branches and, are never so obvious, until the likes of it, now. The trees, once surrounding the world, gave off a greenish glow to prompt the closer galaxies as to our destination but, none responded, and have drifted farther away.

The glow disappeared long times ago. If they were smart, they would have wrapped everything into tiny little baskets, et dit, ciao. One by one, or by orchards, all gave up the ghost. The phenomena, unknown; again, no one wants to go see.

My get-in-the-car and out-of-here routines had partnered and were flawless in technique, only missing one pebbled gully, and a dark cat on the way out. Understand: a pebble will make a stand because it knows it's brothers, a smaller sized vermin will turn around in an unfamiliar area and not cross into the unknown so quickly. A dark cat cares less and is otherwise preoccupied, receiving communications, in coded meowzie, from the loyal swarm moving about the quadrant, and then, pass the script directly to their darkest of masters. The darker, you'll notice, are very different from the others, and a white dot, on the paw's tip indicates extreme intelligence; them understanding ten drop seven two, our segment, and, seven slip four drop echo, our synchrony. For the other, I don't even understand it, and fifteen segments ago I wrote the code.

The outside of my house is perfectly to my liking, opposite and diagonal, a fitted cottage by genre, a white picket posting it's perimeters, with a grey spotted darkling, having arrived by sea and awaiting his underling's presence but, that's before the neighbors fence, and forward propulsion cleared my view. My very small and very liked, and snug, that's creepy sometimes, safety net breaks through the ice's protection

Daddy's home

I noticed the white sheet of paper, as it saluted it's location and under the rocker, which was always beckoning me from my porch gallery; artifacts and oddities gained notoriety amongst the meek, and lessons learned presented a hospitable entryway, but, it was for looks only.

Hands, familiar with the paper's texture; eyes, knowing the meaning of the words appearing before them; my heart laughing at the two big thinkers but

Why was it out here?

Keys were rattled, locks were tacked, and life began again, where walls are nothing, when you're the only one in the room.

Chapter Three

"Blame It On The Noogie"

I refuse to write, anywhere in my work, in any story (with more than two words), where one of my people has the urge to call and give you a phone number to call me back (at). I cannot, in good conscience, break the laws of reality, thus I would be given a triplex of fictitiously created digits, because something other than what will be given me creates ineffectual abundances of the Crown Prince of Annatasia's wardrobe, out of the can, to affect this planets fashion industry for the next millennial, mark slip two.

And, speaking of word processing units, having searchable overtones, and must have been upgraded within the last Squeemer Segment, offering it, you, sorry, a broader range of searching capabilities.

A triple XXX, entered into the engine, might rev a

heartbeat or two, but should not automatically link one to sites a southern woman would scream for at

(+$&#:-(+)
What
(+$&#:-)||+)
The data is right here
(+$&-/#:-)""""+)

You now have a reason for typing dessert into your system, because, now adding an extra X will search for words adjoined in your script; you were working on; a few seconds ago; if you had the upgrade

(CRASHing noise plays)
(+$&#*.*.*.+)
(+*.*.*.+)
You found us
Thank you
To my
Cabinyero
And time keeper
Did you find the update

Obviously, we began oozing outside the mold's measurements from our very beginning and it had to be a ***TalkChat One O Seven at Two***

(**A WHIM**sical, noted stinger plays)

Thanks Tommy

Joining us tonite is Skill Six

(**A SOLO STRATO**magarious discharges)

Who's latest multi platinum discard

Hey

Has let the rockin world get away

In a fog

What the %#\$

Man that ain't cool

Good morning fellas

What kind of #2# you doin Dave

On your ninety four albums

Ninety four

Dude

We just debuted

The extent Six will go to

Six

Skill Six

To put their feet down in it

We're Appetite for Dessert man

Where is he

Can a lifetime subscription

Be paused

I pose the redundant question, knowing the results even before tallied; with, of course, noting, the plus and/or minus percentages left participleling on the end. Their most appreciated participation making the results seem realer

Yes
I believe you

It is not the method by which we survive, that contains our problems, it is the madness within. The feeling of being in a place where nothing is as it should be is so overwhelming, my hips react by instinct and bend my torso forward. The inevitable will happen, smooth landing, or no. Or, if we are the survivors of a past, which should have edumacated today's us to the ways of the self.

We want to be picked up with a line that will surely fulfill our every need to be needed, to have a freshened future for a couple of segments, until hell's constipation begins pushing the stitches to their straining point, leaving us to pander an animotronic freeforall news market, speckled with forty kowlids of growth, while cogs of insistence phlebotomise our system, draining it's aquifers of all it knows and enjoys

I'm old skool

Give me a milkshake from the fountains of my favorite bistro; the one whose menu lists *Chances of Aneurysm*, as one of their multiple choices, instead of the blah, blah, caloric manure it suggests in my dietary protocols. Did have one restaurateur refuse to redo my do, because they were too old to be scared of a werewolf, and so, they failed in their attempt at a flavorful concoction; the straw melted in my hand

I command you to stand
(+$&#+)
(**TIMPANI** rolls)
(***.*.*.**)
Welcome to ***Str8 Off Tha Streetz***
Thank you Dave
Hi everyone
Mister and Missus
Joe
How you doing out there
(**HARMONICA** plays)

I took a breath, raised my bulk from the chair and stepped away from what slowly became blackened paper. The original men of letters, once bold and enlightened, changed through metamorphosis with every breath, the darkened font's dominion replaced by a smokeless ashen dust

Whoa

My reflex, under normal circumstances, is to run, as quickly as possible, to the first available mirror. I don't believe my bloodshot, breathing, elevated pulse, with no funny-looking mists surrounding my cranium, has moved any faster but, there was a short movie flash of a car, with monetary means being dumped into it's bonnet, check. My eyes frantically peered into the background shadows reflecting back to their source, with what looked to be shadow tracers attached, and searched for unwelcome guests. It is a way of life, and a necessity, never knowing who might jump aboard during an exit from the Chamber. Again, check, or, no check, however that can be recorded.

The walls of my smugness materialized smaller today, too. Small in, small out, an old friend used to say; me wondering where my mind had relocated and, why, on the stenopulse that-never-failed, did my musings turn to ash.

Small thoughts, no matter how many, tunneling through a psyche at the very same instant have the inevitable as a future; to meet at the one active terminal along their tracks. Hopefully, one who's directional signal remains operational and absolute.

Whether the convicted is traveling on a ticketless

one-way pass, or has already made the chase to the presumptuous outdoor heaven, and is so mesmerized by the colors of it all, it doubles down on a return stub, which causes it to be summarily conned of their bag of luncheon chips, the crunching noticeably irritating the pain settling behind my eyes. Fate is bound, by rights we give, to lay low and hidden, until it's opportunistic nature can spring on us at just the right time

All such rational thought
Of course

Is contained within luxurious transcontinental railway cars, made with translucent outer shells, and, being soundless on their tracks, steam towards the greatest train wreck to ever be felt in the bones of any man

Doesn't that sound better
Than a bumbling
Intermittent biplane
Buzzing the ear
Make the upgrades

Cyclic activities, for many segments of life, demanded the best that monetary contributions could obtain; it was an ongoing battle not to be comatose. People are generous to a poor guy, who normally awakened on the bottom of a ditch, sometimes amid unknown substances, but, I did learn some things that needed to be known, like:

You are not actually typing letters onto the screen before you. YoU ARE KENetically transforming tiny little squares of nothingness into tints of your charge, and comprehensively etching characteristics into a granite slab that can be neither touched, seen, or retrieved.

With hands impersonating the actions of a trained stenographer, the plucking of secrets remains shielded from the eyes of foreign entities. Your eyes meld together, visionwise *don't get ahead of me* your blurred vision twisting, zigzagging and twisting, until gablelish fire protrudes from the eyes, with a horizontal breath chasing after. This can be done once every octave so, practice on something besides 'A'

Do an 'I'
An 'O'
'Z' is more difficult

Disappearing, my act of weaving words, has always been an interest, both accepted and craved. Replacing a vastness of plain ivory with literaturic scripture became freeing, with words imagined in the opening of a first soliloquy.

When we dream by subsistence, we captivate

everything around us. Our mind's audience, on the edge of their seats, anxiously awaits the next letter of the next phrase to the next paragraph drifting valiantly into its place. The natives do become restless, slamming their jugs of ale together and spilling spirits about, when time and word quiver away

Line please

The word cheap should be out of our vocabulary, by now. If you've ever had a blob of guck poured on you, you'll understand my feelings, when the word is used and associated with us. We, being baba wawa the builder, the commander of quality, have less respect for every other's patriotism, when quality is not given to work given.

We are born, made, and bred locally, and we do not do cheap. And, being made true does not work, if being made wrong is an option. If patriotic quality doesn't concern you, hopefully you're in the upper twenty-one point seven seven percent of the good life. Or, living as a homeless person, for the experience and humblement needed, to know

This is not what I want
But I'm always
Running across this cool stuff

Here's a flashlight. When turned on, it's beam adjusts its strength by the distance of an object in its path; the closer, the softer the beam. In AI mode, circuitry is triggered for it to be controlled by nucleic design, you

Yours is in there

The spread of coverage can be widened, as far as needed, or sharpen it, almost to the edge of a razor, which will be a headline soon

Hacker
Trampled by marauding
Giletto's

There is a laser pointer on the unit, and anything other than that is a creativity exercise for someone else, but not me. But, if someone pulls one of those Chimunga's, now, there will be retaliations

(THE GREATEST FUTURIStic
fighter video plays)
Ok Fine
(LASER BEAM video plays)

The day we look around, and see that stuff is stuff, is the time we realize the importance of us, and, we do that which we have most desired. It is that Pale's Bucket Accumulations urging us to slow down, and possibly, take a break, to quit pushing

Each other

To those who have lived the same history as I, and preach against it, as I also do; bringing into reality the battle of a soul, being raised amongst words no child, regardless of age, should ever hear; and is a warning sign, flashing as a set of memos, and grasped while on maneuvers; them, one step from falling away into the abyss, and me, losing part of the puzzle.

It took all I had, for many years, for the darkness to leave me be. It took even more time to blow the lunar dust off the steno, sit down, and watch reams of paper hauled away during solar waste extraction day, before I'd allow myself the opulence to disappear; my blessing.

In the oddest of ways, my personal battles made me realize that the peace I was missing was already here. So, where was the complaint?

There was no overflow of grace anywhere, and, nor would there be more shuttled to my location. I had had my chance, and had waited the customary two to four weeks for the ordered delivery to arrive safely, but blessings don't end because we have no tags left.

Woke up one morning, on this floor; didn't know

where I was, or how anything got here but, during the first bodily reaction, to my new surroundings, a key fell from my hip and onto the floor, about six micros over there. If, by chance, Gorilla, and his tattooed twin sister, mosied by and had taken off my roof, in four very noisy bites, I don't think their tip-toeing would have been noticed until around Kingsday. And, that is a country mile beyond today's horizons.

I guess I had made it home, with no questions asked. Sometimes, in my zeal to vacate the premises, a few small things are absently deserted. That being, because of the fact that for three years my dilapidation has lived under any facsimile of a roof.

Gladly, on such occasions, there are a few good friends around to help and monetarily compensate my excursions. Them knowing a man's state of mind, and Max knowing a man's ability to tack a lock.

In such an event, Max could scrape together an instrument suitable and necessary for a forgetful one to resume his living conditions, and on occasion, by memory, he says, he can recall the multiple security requirements quantified by my financial institutions regulatory policies.

If mental acuity was a subject needing to be addressed, one might wonder why the mind has begun taking trips to the fantastic but, of course, this is just prior to a sales presentation of our latest craze, Virtual Reaction Golf, being launched

Suit up

The closest anyone gets to the actual game, if not pro carded, is video games. The professional duffers do it live, as they usually always have but, because of some legal technicality involving genetic engineering, the conglomerate, who sanctions the organization's weekly events, lost it's license to hold open tournaments and, just so you know, the amount of politimobiles surrounding the organization, itself, is astounding. VRGolf became an enjoyable and profitable brainchild.

Sure, we did the appropriate gasping to the genetic discoveries thing, but we had heard about their skills and abilities every no-season week of the 'season', before a politio power grew weary of their plight. It was a quandary, which included an eighty five degree wedge, at one hundred ninety micros, with so much backspin torque it left a three meter rooster tail trailing it's dimply behind. When the shot was presented; you'd think arrogance would have had a brain stem; the association was sanctioned into submission. It took generations to make a final impact on the game but, what it changed to was them still making more money than me. And, of course, betting on the outcome of anything not under your full control is, and forever will be, a chance bet.

With the new system, which doesn't work well with animals *yes they tried* we control the ball. Not the ball itself but, more like, what happens to it on it's path towards the indentation on the green.

In my younger years, the enjoyment felt by smacking a ball around for a couple hours couldn't be measured but, eventually, the golden-eyed boys partied too much on the wild side and took it all away. The greens fee remains about the same as playing live, only now, a per round wager can be placed on a hopeful victor. If your chosen one shoots a course record, or, just makes the cut, or not, and has the lowest round of the day, you win the cycle.

Buffs are freely purchased from the pro shop, and depending on your dedication and ability to negotiate, you too could be a championship caliper golfer. All you need is a landscape pod, like mine

A spare is over there
Grab it
Download the buffer
With the guest button
Right there

Three thousand institutionally generated tenders later, a couple leafs, a well-placed tree

Over here
Or right
Over there
That's good

You're almost set. If you want to go neck deep in your investment, purchase that rain-making cloud, right

There you go

The only unsanctioned element is the wind. However, many failed experiments have been performed to capture creationist items, and many spouses have been frustrated, because their awesome other lacks the ability to not exude a sheet of saliva over the Pinnacle's screen.

It did become apparent, to the apparently empowered, to unfund all experiments pertaining to the existence of air. As a side note, their efforts, along with tag along input from various cospiritors, made the art of whistling criminal. So, a new formation of windless sequential deoxy was created, generating a new fold of choice players. In other words, genetically coded nationalists picked up a club for the first time; the process became operational.

A cloud is a natural element, and not a single 'noid has ever cornered the market on weather makers, except clouds, which is a good question for tomorrow's philosophical science quiz

Can a cloud be monopolized

But, conditions must be exact for moisture to accumulate within a nimbolic structure, causing rain, naturally. And, there is so much competition in the sky already, placing fluffy formations into the game is leaning more towards overkill than anything else. If it's going to shower anyways, it's cheaper to go au naturale. Nonetheless, I do not appreciate the IT sales guys popping one into the air, every so often; so, maybe I'll think about being blindly sucked into their scheme, again. I didn't become a Sychicseer before buying one but, by reviewing their properties, the puffy little cooler magnets are best thrown back into the game, during a rainstorm

Pick your player
From the lobby over there
Take your time

It's day four, and the cut hasn't been made yet, and that one leaning at the bar came in fifth last week. He always looks like

Ok
Pick that one
He'll do you good
And, yes
Thank you for your referral

I'm just reading an email. I get points, and a free buff for you being my guest and playing along. When you finally make it out on the course; it really is a rite of passage; to use your buffs, push that button

There you go
Thank you for your purchase
And
Thank you again for playing
I get points for that too
No more
Promise
Until halftime

When you're out on the course, use the buffs to screw around with every other player involved in the tournament. With the understanding that there are those others, who are tweaking at your player, also

You Thirsty
Sure
In the fridge
Leave three tenders in the tower of
death beside the condenser

It's entertaining to partake in an addiction, and watch the pros expressions, while a sudden and unexpected tree blooms across their path

That button there

Gets you a mammoth of a sprout, it's called Mabel. She's a giant and

Cannot be placed
Within twenty micros of the fairways
Or greens

And, never rooted within fifty micros of the tee; which is considered unfair, by standards; it would interfere with the ball's trajectory. That doesn't mean you can't mortgage your house and plant the behemoth, that has a radius hundreds of micros wide at seed, then, it's limbs spread to hell and back over the fairways. Here it is

> *Mabel must be purchased*
> *And placed at least a fathom*
> *In advance of tournaments*

So that they can take hold and not topple over and onto the non-participating VR gallery. Controllers are not allowed on course.

If you can guess where your ball, or theirs, is going to land on the green, after traveling through a gauntlet, you are more than encouraged to use, at your leisure, the free backspin buff.

On an average approach, by the time your ball, with revolutionary actions created by a player's swing, tops it's apex, another competitor's actions has, more than likely, made the dimpled medallion a dead weight, and, by process of elimination, a weapon. Getting it to spin again, without affecting its trajectory, which has already been compromised, is almost impossible.

There are no penalties for water hazards, so, when, or if, your ball lands on the green, your controller can now be used to channel, or coax the ball towards the hole. But, considering the laws of Physics, even these days, with every action and so forth, counter actions of counter actions are a must; another gamer is teaching your ball to do tricks and travel in a direction not beneficial to your game. And, while your frustrations break into pieces worthless material items, skill will replace dumb luck when you've paid your dues

Sumbitch

A wise-ass, named Petris, took advantage of the wind, and the discount prices, to toss an elephant ear into my path. Needless to say, my ball, having no choice and little grace, died on impact, falling well short of the green. And yes, it gets bad when a leaf carries a physics book. I laugh, as the beginning clicker of a movie started projecting some guy's idea of how to create enough topspin to cause a ball to seek out an extra inch or two, on it's beleaguered fairway run

A competitor
Engaged in tournament competition
Cannot enhance his player's shot
Causing forward motion to same
Unless ball is on a green
For your overkill
Moment of the day
No item's travel
Shall not be hindered
Or altered

If a ball is put into motion from a tee, and strikes any object on course grounds succeeding launch, items contact will be considered unnatural in nature. If an in-play ball creates motion, of any kind, within any unnatural item thereof, all contracts with presumed unnatural items will be placed into void status

You can then throw
It in the receptacle
With the rest of the singing group
And hope for a new melody

You wanted me to read it.

If you're not into imploding in on yourself, stay away from the tee boxes. I've seen many looks, when the ball lands in the fork of a tree

A one-stroke penalty
With no drop

Or, when he or she doesn't want to blame himerself, or the ball, for the shot just made. Their eyes are like my reflected shadows from earlier; on fire, cold and lifeless.

There have been many champions, as in any time but, equally, the greatest of the greatest, of all time, lose their luster after an eon, or two. It is within our lifetime that our natural heroes are able to be touched and seen, and cheered for. They play the games we love, the enjoyments we are dedicated to and, it is us who triumphantly hoist the trophy for posting a winning score

When Neosun
Fell from the sky
Did it make a sound

It did, actually; a high-pitched whistle, as it went streaking by. It became a comical endeavor, with the projected finger transmitted to its surface, while passing. We call the failure, TeNSdIP: The Night Science Dumped It's Pants. They didn't know it was coming and exactly what a person wants to hear, when Straton makes the same trek a little over three hundred years later

Ever lay your head
Over to one side
And go
Huh

The words universe, or solar system, for some; might mean me, might mean my neighbor, whom

I sat with
When he saw the story
About the octopus
And still he believes
(**THE HIGHEST PITCHED** voice plays)
It's all fake
And do
(**THROaT** clearing plays)
(**REGULAR** voice plays)
And don't ask

If a mind is not full of the idea that we are really grains of dust, living on a wet rock, which is floating aimlessly through the same space as one hundred billion other galaxies. If a person does not accept this, they have not sat down and studied the all encompassing space we exist in, or their river runs only so far, and, any farther would mean a total collapse of reality, of their world. When you can calibrate your calculations spool, follow that beam from my new flashlight, and do it for a light-year. When you get to the end and Grump it back, another forty-six times; that's, 5.879 times 10 to the 12th power, in miles. And, just to belabour the point, do you think a grain of sand is laying out on the beach, thinking it's the suds of suds?

We get ourselves in most problems, because we

believe we are it. We can't jump tall buildings on Ole Poots Day, or tricycle through the badlands, or, the most telling sign of all, sneaker dance with one of the Shams; and, I couldn't do that, if my life depended on it.

We look out into the skies, hoping it will all be alright, for one, but, what is seen is a spec of matter, sometimes, no bigger than the stone beneath our feet. It's difficult to grasp perspective, when one is unable to see the forest, for the trees in the way.

Life on other planets has been a financial investment opportunity, made especially for those who have too much money, that's not theirs, and not enough travel miles to warrant Changri Le. But, that could just be me.

Why do we concern ourselves with others, when we can't resolve our own issues with each other. If an alien ship were to land, and the ancient tribe of Triplets, who were disturbed by the arrival, automatically split their pair of eights

(**TRIBAL** AWWW plays)

There will be nothing our leaders will be able to do, after tracking the ship to its landing area. Actually, there was a rumor going around about a vehicular object, sitting over a couple blocks. The alien among us, having skidded in on an emergency stop, leaped from an opening in the craft's shell, started screaming, and ran down the alley. It turned out to be a scream of glee; BubbaRibs was back.

The greed of politics has never changed, and manipulation and image remain to be words to live by. Petitioners, centuries ago, voted to limit political ads and the speaking of it, from any candidate, to only two months during an election year. We stuck a cork in it.

I realized, it has been my generation obtaining the positions of power, which is what they wanted in their youth; protesting against anything not nailed down or shut; and, without exception, individually stood before the multitudes, proclaiming Providence by their hand, and then they slithered behind locked doors and traded our souls for the most useless, most impractical devices.

They were to create a utilitarian society fitting to us but, all they doubly produced was a demographic suitable to themselves, and barren lands stretching for billions of hectares.

It is our gene pool, who is now influencing, training, and leading our predecessor generations, so that when they mature and come of age, as we needed to, they will be ready to take their shot at the big picture.

As a politimobile, what they're referred to in our media, if you had a good story, or your opponent didn't, you could catch the aye of a storm, bolstering it with lies, gladly accepted by too many, which, never really made sense to me but, it guaranteed an induction into the grappling hall of fame, which is just a wall. In order to take a position upon it, you must first

Be extraordinary in efforts
To propel humanity into the outer
Regions of completion
Don't leave
And affix to humanity
Applications beneficial to the
Attainment of products
Satisfactorily distributed
End quote

That's right out of the manual, by the way and

Mother never
Mentioned any of this

My eyes felt pitted behind their lids, an effect brought on by the daggers of light, bluntly stabbing them in their backs. And, at some point; hopefully, time hasn't sped up; the sun has syphoned its way to Frisday. Max said it was, and that myself had been here on schedule, and the stranger things got. My body trembled.

He was now down that way, introducing a new

protege to the clan; an act normally observed on less frequently attended days, so as to not overload already stressed reactionary pods on the day of baptism.

The atmosphere of the Chamber did not only condition new patrons to their surroundings, the rugrats also appeared in the nooks and crannies only accessible to those behind the counter. By their witness, our spiritual proprietors came in all shapes and sizes, caused havoc at any moment and, oddly enough, never acted up in front of customers, except for those drowning their sorrows. So, they made the scene, when profitable, but normally gravitated to the boxes in the cooler. Leading me to believe, hell is not the hot, boiling metropolis below us, as we picture it in our thoughts and scriptures. It's in my neighbor's attic, with an open bar and plenty of Sunshine. Moonlight. Good times.

Speaking of a tandem trio, there are three years in my life that can't be accounted for. The sum total of the memory panel shows me drinking for four of it, during which time, apparently, the hex finally became as exhausted as me. By the by, if you ever have an opportunity to search for a thought that doesn't exist, good luck. Since the witchery, my hands have broken the seal on every bottle, except when here, of course, but, what has happened in and to the last couple of days has the worrisome meter working overtime.

"Thank you, Max"

His sense of his surroundings is beyond reproach, and that's whether or not he's tending bar, or developing his balancing skills on one of the stools on this side. Regardless, there were always the street sirens in the downtown area to keep things lively.

Their so-called wailing sounds like pigeons cooing, which, became extent after the pro golf scandal *don't ask I'm not saying a thing* and, bless the poor child who will be made sacrifice as a result of pulling such a stupid thieving stunt. In the downtown area, at that.

No signs are posted, and no metallic security badges, warning discretion, are displayed in the store windows. After all, no laws are broken, that would be objected to, anyways.

This procedure was drafted by GAP and our leaders, to stymie the law breakers.

The culprits penance will be given as a gift to a god who longer exists *again please don't ask* it hasn't been a very good year. My worry, along with every other breather, including a very powerful primate community, is when they start searching house to house and, what will they be looking for when they're all out of idiots?

We, as a Chamber, don't exist past the bell, as far as anyone is concerned. Our bodies reside here, under the control of the peppermint squad, quietly perusing our fate, hoping they don't discover that we think we're smarter than they are. Stealthy things they are too, but, now that we've broached the subject, Max said there was a stranger come in the other day, and the spooks never came out, which has the place a little on edge. They're always here but they are always here when virgins are near. And, yes, I don't mean that literally.

He was a regular looking guy, with no outward attributes any different than any other regular guy, who happened to be new, and taking notes. None of the shelf proclaimed psychics blew circuitry upon his arrival, or, during what he might have needed to be a streaming broadcast nite.

Maybe the boogie night crew spent too much time in the cooler and were singing that new year's song they loved so much but, you couldn't tell unless you were almost on them; quiet for the customers, you know. Maybe the regular guy is not so regular after all, and has a Delk-Cranien-niff-ca-fartum on him and, I don't care why, either. I will tell you, Max doesn't get around here pretty quick, I'll have to have conversations with his bosses and just in time, the newbie-wan replaces my empty with another moistened towelette.

I tipped my glass, thanking the energetic for their participation. She held her polite smile, while returning her attention to the gathering of dishes, when a friend of the bar poked its headish-looking object out from its home away from home, stretching to sniff the girls devilishly attractive auburn hair

Shoo

Was a panic stricken person's first reaction, and louder than intended, and surely, something a future spouse would be offended by but, unlike the Chamber, the spooks, again, never reacted to noise; red hair, evidently, got the juices flowing

Lucky ghost

Bodies turned, reactions and observations were acknowledged, calm remained, with my swatting at a mysterious flying thing fluttering about my territory. A slight wave would have sufficed but, under the circumstances, the mellow-dramatic worked best, but, didn't that head jump?

Max was, again, off somewhere, talking about ape politics shhh *somewhere along your way we traced it back to your time so listen you have a madman about to obtain dinosaur dna from a mosquito* thereby recreating the species for amusement purposes *you have to do something for me it won't cost much don't leave it will be worth it there's a guy who will not survive his outing he is my uncle and you must save him from dying in that toilet.*

If you wanna have an intelligent conversation, talk to a monkey. They'll be more than happy to tell you all about themselves, and their plight. And, how some fool typed a thread of knowledge into a chain of events that caused the world to roll over in its grave. The population explosion, following this genetically enhanced endeavor, with a bit of human brilliance tossed in to fuel the fire, became even greater than when a platypus graduated with a doctorate, and is now Chancellor of some school of higher learning back east. Since, legislation has been enacted, where non-humans are not allowed to vote, or hold office. Anyone who is anyone has yet to answer the questions, why is the sky falling, and why are members of the orangutan clan being elected during every new term of parliament. And, why am I having this conversation!

The banana nut's power and resilience is more evident in each remake of a long-lived documentary and biography, which stars genetically engineered primates, and documents an evolutionary change within themselves. The ending is always the same, with them becoming a better us.

Whatever is setting the chunk of cheese in the traps outside, and is pulling the sacrifices from the streets and is not concerned with such a petty foolishness, as politics, is making me nervous.

If the thieves were worth a pecos a dozen, there would be an offering from our kind to the altar but they, them, those ones, who follow this new religion have no spirit and never have need of monetary increases. We do worry about such things because, you may never know who the regular guy will be, or, who he will not be, and with the regular guys having a lack of spirit, which is alarming to our locals, there might be need of a time to set off silent alarms around us all, but, a magnetic transference of the predestined reveals *it's you guys stop it if you think it's bad now wait till you have nothing to hang stripes on.*

At a point in time, fifty seven slip six segments, mach three naught two nanoseconds, elevation nine, to be precise, a humanoid figure will come to ask a favor of you. In his hands will be a vial containing a schematic of the new human condition; it must be inserted post haste into the glutomus maxelmus. If you receive responsibility for this destiny changing formula, which alters *again* a chromosome connected to our evolution and returns it to its original base fraction, phantoms of every kind will cease their progression within our being and return us to a most original state of consciousness.

While fulfilling your assignment, you will erase mankind's errors made within our genetic tree, nullifying the mistakes of past manipulators, who are bent on filtering their example of pure material into a code that we will be bound to live by. It is clear, as to what will happen, if your opportunity is refused. If it is not clear, as to what will be the future of us and you have monetary investment in the aforementioned scripture, put this work down, immediately, you have the wrong edition. Return to the location of your purchase, and buy a differing copy of these same paragraphs, clearly marked with an obscure 'X'. During your quest, my person will be lifted up from its place of internment, and float listlessly toward yon doorway

Guess you could say
I gotta go number two

My adieu bids you fondly.
Make life enjoyable.